Rick S

P9-DBQ-960

POCKET AMSTERDAM

Rick Steves & Gene Openshaw

Contents

Introduction 3
Amsterdam City Walk 13
Rijksmuseum Tour 35
Van Gogh Museum Tour 53
Red Light District Walk 69
Jordaan Walk 85
Anne Frank House Tour 101
Sights 113
Sleeping 137
Eating 143
Practicalities 155
Index 179

Introduction

Amsterdam of the Golden Age (the 1600s) was the world's richest city. And it's still a wonderland of canals, stately brick mansions, and carillons chiming from church spires. Today's Amsterdam is a progressive place of 820,000 people and almost as many bikes. Visitors will find no end of world-class sights: Van Gogh's *Sunflowers,* Rembrandt's self-portraits, and Anne Frank's secret hiding place.

Enjoy the city's intimate charms. Stroll quiet neighborhoods, browse bookshops, sample exotic foods, and let a local show you the right way to swallow a pickled herring. With legal marijuana and prostitution, Amsterdam exudes an earthy spirit of live and let live. Consider yourself warned...or titillated. Take it all in, then pause to watch the clouds blow past gabled rooftops—and see the Golden Age reflected in a quiet canal.

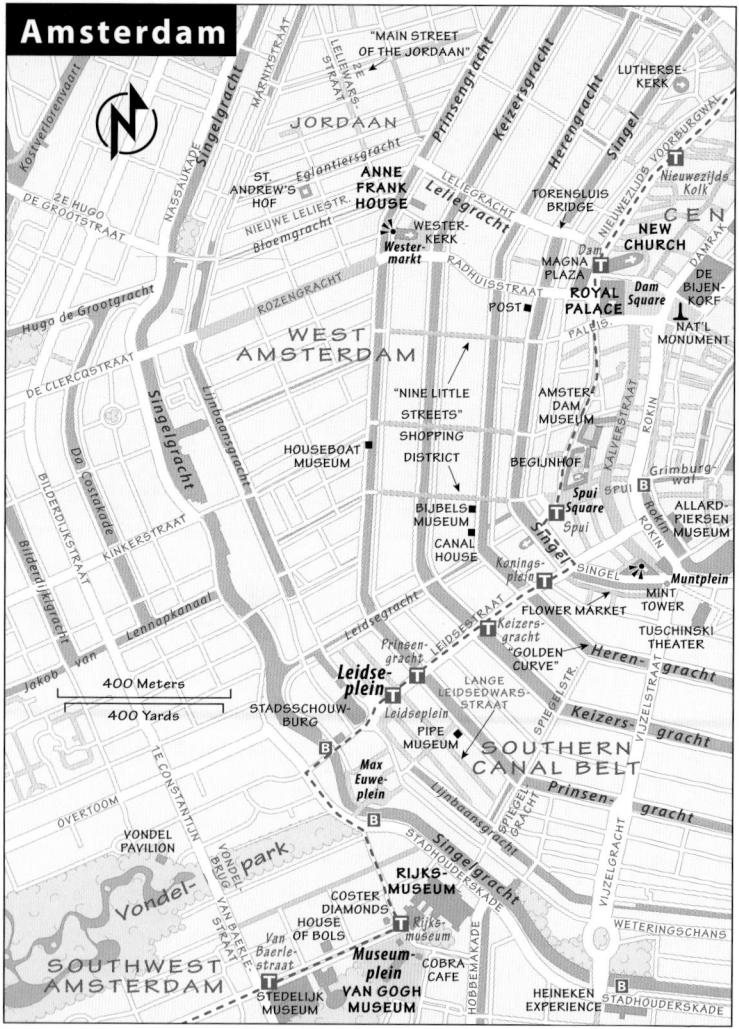
Amsterdam
"MAIN STREET OF THE JORDAAN"
JORDAAN
Prinsengracht
Keizersgracht
Herengracht
Singel
Lelliegracht
Eglantiersgracht
Bloemgracht
Westermarkt
Hugo de Grootgracht
Singelgracht
Kostverlorenvaart
Lijnbaansgracht
Lennepkanaal
Jakob van Bilderdijkgracht
Leidsegracht
Prinsengracht
Keizersgracht
"GOLDEN CURVE"
Heerengracht
Keizersgracht
Prinsengracht
Singelgracht
Vondelpark
WEST AMSTERDAM
SOUTHERN CANAL BELT
SOUTHWEST AMSTERDAM
CENTRUM
ANNE FRANK HOUSE
ST. ANDREW'S HOF
WESTERKERK
LUTHERSE KERK
TORENSLUIS BRIDGE
NEW CHURCH
MAGNA PLAZA
ROYAL PALACE
Dam Square
DE BIJENKORF
NAT'L MONUMENT
POST
"NINE LITTLE STREETS" SHOPPING DISTRICT
AMSTERDAM MUSEUM
HOUSEBOAT MUSEUM
BEGIJNHOF
Spui Square
ALLARD PIERSON MUSEUM
BIJBELS MUSEUM
CANAL HOUSE
Koningsplein
Muntplein
MINT TOWER
FLOWER MARKET
TUSCHINSKI THEATER
Leidseplein
LANGE LEIDSEDWARSSTRAAT
STADSSCHOUWBURG
PIPE MUSEUM
Max Euweplein
RIJKSMUSEUM
COSTER DIAMONDS
HOUSE OF BOLS
Rijksmuseum
Museumplein
VAN GOGH MUSEUM
COBRA CAFE
STEDELIJK MUSEUM
HEINEKEN EXPERIENCE
VONDEL PAVILION
400 Meters
400 Yards

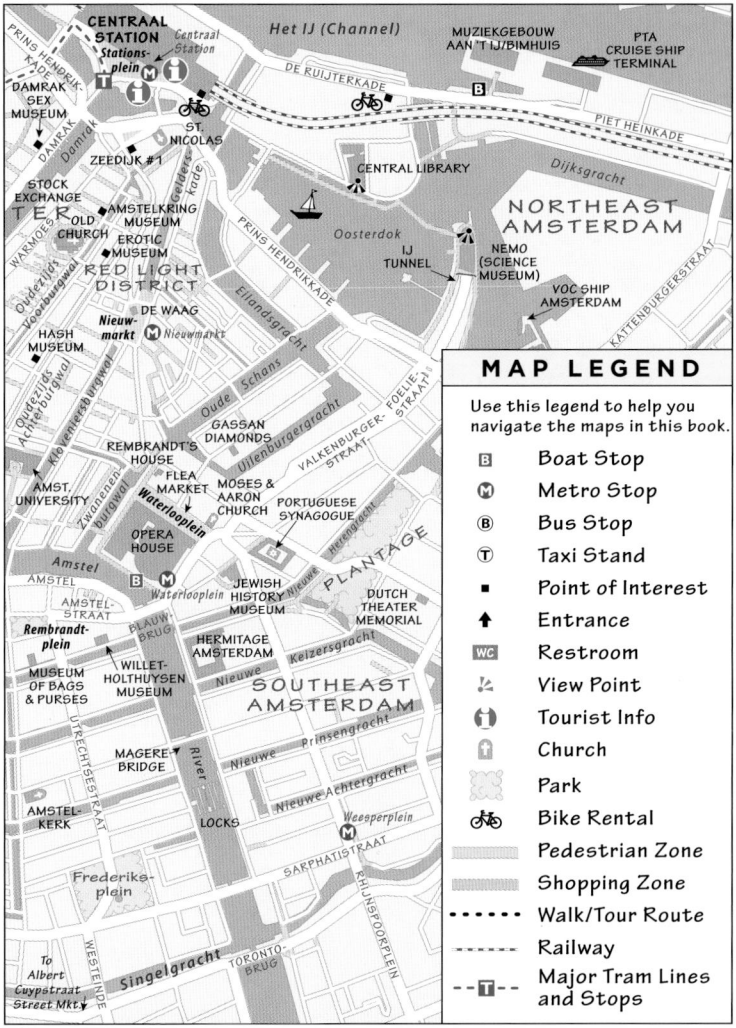
CENTRAAL STATION
Stations-plein
Centraal Station
Het IJ (Channel)
MUZIEKGEBOUW AAN 'T IJ/BIMHUIS
PTA CRUISE SHIP TERMINAL
PRINS HENDRIKKADE
DE RUIJTERKADE
DAMRAK SEX MUSEUM
DAMRAK
Damrak
ST. NICOLAS
PIET HEINKADE
ZEEDIJK #1
Oudezijds Kolk
CENTRAL LIBRARY
Dijksgracht
STOCK EXCHANGE
TER
AMSTELKRING MUSEUM
OLD CHURCH
EROTIC MUSEUM
WARMOES
NORTHEAST AMSTERDAM
Oosterdok
PRINS HENDRIKKADE
IJ TUNNEL
NEMO (SCIENCE MUSEUM)
RED LIGHT DISTRICT
Oudezijds Voorburgwal
Ellandsgracht
VOC SHIP AMSTERDAM
KATTENBURGERSTRAAT
DE WAAG
Nieuwmarkt
Nieuwmarkt
HASH MUSEUM
Oude Schans
Oudezijds Achterburgwal
Oude Zijds Voorburgwal
GASSAN DIAMONDS
Uilenburgergracht
VALKENBURGERSTRAAT
FOELIESTRAAT
REMBRANDT'S HOUSE
FLEA MARKET
MOSES & AARON CHURCH
AMST. UNIVERSITY
Zwanenburgwal
Waterlooplein
PORTUGUESE SYNAGOGUE
Herengracht
OPERA HOUSE
PLANTAGE
Amstel
AMSTEL
Waterlooplein
JEWISH HISTORY MUSEUM
Nieuwe
DUTCH THEATER MEMORIAL
AMSTELSTRAAT
Rembrandtplein
PLAUWBRUG
HERMITAGE AMSTERDAM
Keizersgracht
MUSEUM OF BAGS & PURSES
WILLET-HOLTHUYSEN MUSEUM
Nieuwe
SOUTHEAST AMSTERDAM
UTRECHTSESTRAAT
MAGERE BRIDGE
River
Nieuwe Prinsengracht
Nieuwe Achtergracht
AMSTEL-KERK
LOCKS
Weesperplein
SARPHATISTRAAT
Frederiksplein
RHIJNSPOORPLEIN
To Albert Cuypstraat Street Mkt.
WESTERPLEIN
Singelgracht
TORONTOBRUG
MAP LEGEND
Use this legend to help you navigate the maps in this book.
Boat Stop
Metro Stop
Bus Stop
Taxi Stand
Point of Interest
Entrance
Restroom
View Point
Tourist Info
Church
Park
Bike Rental
Pedestrian Zone
Shopping Zone
Walk/Tour Route
Railway
Major Tram Lines and Stops

About This Book

With this book, I've selected only the best of Amsterdam—admittedly, a tough call. The core of the book is six self-guided tours that zero in on Amsterdam's greatest sights and neighborhoods. The Amsterdam City Walk takes you through the heart of the city, giving you the lay of the land. At the Rijksmuseum and Van Gogh Museum, you'll see all the essentials with time left over for browsing. You'll go window-shopping in the racy Red Light District, meander the tree-lined canals of the Jordaan, and visit the Anne Frank House for insight into her tragic—but ultimately uplifting—story.

The rest of the book is a traveler's tool kit. You'll find plenty more about Amsterdam's attractions, from shopping to nightlife to less touristy sights. And there are helpful hints on saving money, avoiding crowds, getting around on Amsterdam's trams, finding a great meal, and much more.

If you'd like more information than this Pocket Guide offers, I've sprinkled the book liberally with Web references. For general travel tips—as well as updates for this book—see www.ricksteves.com.

Amsterdam by Neighborhood

Amsterdam's Centraal station sits on the north edge of the city. From here, the city spreads out like a fan in a series of concentric canals. Damrak is

Key to This Book

Sights are rated:

▲▲▲ **Don't miss**
▲▲ **Try hard to see**
▲ **Worthwhile if you can make it**
No rating **Worth knowing about**

Tourist information offices are abbreviated as **TI,** and bathrooms are **WC**s.

Like Europe, this book uses the **24-hour clock.** It's the same through 12:00 noon, then keeps going: 13:00, 14:00, and so on.

For **opening times,** if a sight is listed as "May-Oct daily 9:00-16:00," it's open from 9 a.m. until 4 p.m. from the first day of May until the last day of October (but expect exceptions).

the main north-south axis, connecting Centraal station with Dam Square, the city's main square. Farther south are Leidseplein (nightlife) and the major museums (Rijksmuseum and Van Gogh).

To walk north-south through the sightseeing core—from Centraal station to Dam Square to Leidseplein to the Rijksmuseum—takes about an hour.

Think of Amsterdam as a series of neighborhoods, cradling major landmarks.

Central Amsterdam: The historic core runs from Centraal station along Damrak, passing through two major city squares (Dam and Spui) and ending at the Mint Tower. The central spine of streets (Damrak,

Amsterdam at a Glance

▲▲▲ **Rijksmuseum** Best collection anywhere of the Dutch Masters—Rembrandt, Hals, Vermeer, and Steen—in a spectacular setting. **Hours:** Daily 9:00-17:00. See page 35.

▲▲▲ **Van Gogh Museum** More than 200 paintings by the angst-ridden artist. **Hours:** Daily 9:00-18:00 (mid-July-Aug until 19:00), Fri until 22:00, Sat until 21:00 in mid-July-Aug. See page 53.

▲▲▲ **Anne Frank House** Young Anne's hideaway during the Nazi occupation. **Hours:** April-Oct daily 9:00-22:00, Nov-March daily 9:00-19:00, Sat until 21:00. See page 101.

▲▲ **Stedelijk Museum** The Netherlands' top modern-art museum, recently and extensively renovated. **Hours:** Daily 10:00-18:00, Fri until 22:00. See page 123.

▲▲ **Vondelpark** City park and concert venue. See page 124.

▲▲ **Amsterdam Museum** City's growth from fishing village to trading capital to today, including some Rembrandts and a playable carillon. **Hours:** Daily 10:00-17:00. See page 118.

▲▲ **Amstelkring Museum** Catholic church hidden in the attic of a 17th-century merchant's house. **Hours:** Mon-Sat 10:00-17:00, Sun 13:00-17:00. See page 118.

▲▲ **Red Light District Walk** Women of the world's oldest profession on the job. **Hours:** Best from noon into the evening; avoid late at night. See page 69.

▲▲ **Netherlands Maritime Museum** Rich seafaring story of the Netherlands, told with vivid artifacts. **Hours:** Daily 9:00-17:00. See page 133.

▲▲ **Hermitage Amsterdam** Russia's Tsarist treasures, on loan from St. Petersburg. **Hours:** Daily 10:00-17:00. See page 129.

▲▲ **Dutch Resistance Museum** History of the Dutch struggle against the Nazis. **Hours:** Tue-Fri 10:00-17:00, Sat-Mon 11:00-17:00. See page 132.

▲ **Museumplein** Square with art museums, street musicians, crafts, and nearby diamond demos. See page 123.

▲ **Leidseplein** Lively square with cafés and street musicians. **Hours:** Always open, best on sunny afternoons. See page 125.

▲ **Royal Palace** Lavish City Hall that takes you back to the Golden Age of the 17th century. **Hours:** Daily 11:00-17:00 when not closed for official ceremonies. See page 116.

▲ **Begijnhof** Quiet courtyard lined with picturesque houses. **Hours:** Daily 8:00-17:00. See page 116.

▲ **Hash, Marijuana, and Hemp Museum** All the dope, from history and science to memorabilia. **Hours:** Daily 10:00-22:00. See page 84.

▲ **EYE Film Institute Netherlands** Film museum and cinema complex housed in a futuristic building. **Hours:** Exhibits open daily 10:00-19:00, cinemas and bar open roughly 10:00-24:00. See page 134.

▲ **Rembrandt's House** The master's reconstructed house, displaying his etchings. **Hours:** Daily 10:00-18:00. See page 128.

▲ **Diamond Tours** Offered at shops throughout the city. **Hours:** Generally daily 9:00-17:00. See page 129.

▲ **Willet-Holthuysen Museum** Elegant 17th-century house. **Hours:** Mon-Fri 10:00-17:00, Sat-Sun from 11:00. See page 126.

▲ **Jewish Historical Museum and Portuguese Synagogue** Exhibits on Judaism and culture and beloved synagogue that serves today's Jewish community. **Hours:** Daily 11:00-17:00. See page 130.

▲ **Dutch Theater** Moving memorial in former Jewish detention center. **Hours:** Daily 11:00-17:00. See page 131.

▲ **Tropical Museum** Re-creations of tropical-life scenes. **Hours:** Daily 10:00-17:00, closed Mon off-season. See page 132.

Houseboat Museum Your chance to see one of these floating homes from the inside. **Hours:** March-Oct Tue-Sun 11:00-17:00, closed Mon; Nov-Dec and Feb Fri-Sun 11:00-17:00, closed Mon-Thu; closed most of Jan. See page 120.

Central Library Architecturally fun spot—with great view terrace—to take a breather among Amsterdam's bookworms. **Hours:** Daily 10:00-22:00. See page 133.

Kalverstraat, Rokin) has some of the city's main department, chain, and tourist stores. To the east of Damrak is the city's oldest area (today's Red Light District) and the revitalized waterfront around the train station.

West Amsterdam: West of Damrak is a pleasant area known for its four grand, tree-lined canals. Here you'll find the Anne Frank House, boutique shops, and many of my recommended hotels and restaurants. Farther west is the quieter, cozier (and mostly residential) Jordaan neighborhood.

Southern Canal Belt: The next ring of canals south of the historic core is spacious and dotted sparsely with a few intimate museums, art galleries, antique shops, and recommended B&Bs. Rowdy Leidseplein anchors the lower corner.

Southwest Amsterdam: The city's major art museums (Rijksmuseum, Van Gogh, Stedelijk) and other sights cluster together on an expansive square, Museumplein. A short walk away is Vondelpark, Amsterdam's version of a central park. While less central, Southwest Amsterdam is easily reached by tram, so I've recommended some good-value hotels.

Southeast Amsterdam: Stretching from the edge of the Old City Center to the very outskirts, this neighborhood has a number of interesting sights, especially in the former Jewish Quarter. You'll find Rembrandt's House, a flea market, the Hermitage Amsterdam, and several Jewish-themed sights. Farther southeast (accessible by tram) are some Nazi-era sights, a zoo, and a botanical garden.

Northeast Amsterdam: East of Centraal station is the newly revitalized waterfront, with the Central Library, the Netherlands Maritime Museum, and a children's science museum (NEMO).

Planning Your Time

The following day-plans give an idea of how much an organized, motivated, and caffeinated person can see. Amsterdam deserves at least three full sightseeing days.

Day 1: Follow my self-guided Amsterdam City Walk, leading from the train station to Leidseplein. After lunch, visit Amsterdam's two outstanding art museums, located next to each other: the Van Gogh Museum and the Rijksmuseum. In the evening, stroll the Red Light District for some memorable window-shopping.

Day 2: Start your day with a one-hour canal boat tour. Then visit

Daily Reminder

The biggest Amsterdam sights—the Rijksmuseum, the Van Gogh Museum, and the Anne Frank House—are open daily year-round (except the Anne Frank House, which closes for Yom Kippur).

Sunday: These sights have limited, afternoon-only hours today—the Amstelkring Museum (13:00-17:00) and Old Church (13:00-17:00). The Canal House, Westerkerk church and tower, and the Old Church tower are closed altogether, as is the Waterlooplein flea market.

Monday: The Houseboat Museum, Canal House, the Old Church tower, and Tropical Museum are closed today. From September through May, NEMO is closed today (but open in peak season). Many businesses are closed Monday morning.

Tuesday: All recommended sights are open, except the Old Church tower. The Houseboat Museum is closed off-season.

Wednesday: All recommended sights are open, except the Old Church tower. The Houseboat Museum is closed off-season.

Thursday: All recommended sights are open. The Stedelijk Museum is open until 22:00. The Houseboat Museum is closed off-season.

Friday: The Van Gogh Museum is open until 22:00.

Saturday: The Anne Frank House is open until 22:00 mid-March-mid-Sept, and until 21:00 in the off-season.

Late-Night Sightseeing: The Anne Frank House stays open daily July-Aug until 22:00. The city's naughty sights are open late every day: the Hash, Marijuana, and Hemp Museum until 22:00, the Damrak Sex Museum until 23:00, and the Erotic Museum until midnight or later.

the sights of your choice around Rembrandtplein (Rembrandt's house, Waterlooplein flea market, Gassan Diamonds polishing demo, Dutch Resistance Museum). In the evening, tour the Anne Frank House and take my self-guided Jordaan Walk before enjoying dinner in that neighborhood.

Day 3: Use this day to browse the wide variety of Amsterdam's museums—the Amstelkring, Royal Palace, Stedelijk, Bags and Purses, Pipes, and Houseboat.

With more time: There are plenty more small museums to visit in Amsterdam—find suggestions in the Sights chapter. Or day-trip to nearby towns such as Haarlem, Delft, or Edam.

These are busy day-plans, so be sure to schedule in slack time for picnics, laundry, people-watching, leisurely dinners, shopping, and recharging your touristic batteries. Slow down and be open to unexpected experiences and the courtesy of the Dutch people.

Quick Tips: Here are a few tips to get you started. (You'll find more information on these topics throughout the book.) Reserve your hotel as soon as is feasible, because Amsterdam is crowded from mid-March through September. To avoid long lines, book exactly two months in advance for your visit to the Anne Frank House. Consider also buying tickets in advance for the Rijksmuseum and Van Gogh Museum. Since opening hours are variable, get the latest information from museum websites, at **www.iamsterdam.com,** or from local publications when you arrive. A sightseeing pass, which covers admission to many sights and lets you skip ticket-buying lines, can be worthwhile for busy sightseers. 🎧 Take advantage of my free Amsterdam audio tours, covering many of this book's sights. (For more details, see page 167.)

And finally, remember that although Amsterdam's sights can be crowded and stressful, the city itself is all about gentility and grace, so...be flexible.

Have a great trip!

Amsterdam City Walk

From Centraal Station to Leidseplein

Take a Dutch sampler walk from one end of the old center to the other, tasting all that Amsterdam has to offer along the way. It's your best single stroll through quintessentially Dutch scenes, hidden churches, surprising shops, thriving happy-hour hangouts, and eight centuries of history.

The walk starts at Centraal station, heads down touristy Damrak to Dam Square, and continues south down pedestrian-only Kalverstraat to the Mint Tower. Then it wafts through the flower market, before continuing south to busy Leidseplein. To return to Centraal station, catch tram #2 or #5 from Leidseplein.

ORIENTATION

Length of This Walk: About three miles—allow three hours.
When to Go: Best by day, when sights are open.
Alert: Beware of silent trams (don't walk on tracks) and yield to bikes.
Royal Palace: €10, daily 10:00-17:00 but often closed for official business.
New Church: Free to view from gift-shop balcony, interior with special exhibits-€8-15, audioguide-€3, daily 10:00-17:00.
De Papegaai Hidden Church: Free, Mon-Sat 10:00-16:00, Sun until 14:00.
Amsterdam Museum: €12.50, daily 10:00-17:00.
Civic Guards Gallery: Free, daily 10:00-17:00.
Begijnhof: Free, daily 8:00-17:00.
Tours: 🎧 Download my free Amsterdam City Walk audio tour.
Services: You can find WCs at fast-food places, near the entrance to the Amsterdam Museum, and in the Kalvertoren shopping mall.

THE WALK BEGINS

❶ Centraal Station

Here, where today's train travelers enter the city, sailors of yore disembarked from seagoing ships. They were met by street musicians, pickpockets, hotel runners, and ladies carrying red lanterns. Centraal station, built in the late 1800s, sits on reclaimed land at what was once the harbor mouth. With warm red brick and prickly spires, the station is the first of several Neo-Gothic buildings we'll see from the late-19th century, the era of Amsterdam's economic revival. One of the station's towers has a clock dial; the other tower's dial is a weather vane. Watch the hand twitch as the wind gusts in every direction—N, Z, O, and W.

Let's get oriented: *noord, zuid, oost,* and *west.* Facing the station, you're facing north. Farther north, on the other side of the station, is the IJ (pronounced "eye"), the body of water that gives Amsterdam access to the open sea.

Now turn your back to the station and face the city, looking south. The city spreads out before you like a fan, in a series of concentric canals. Ahead of you stretches the street called Damrak, which leads to Dam Square a half-mile away. That's where we're headed.

To the left of Damrak is the city's old *(oude)* town. More recently, that

Centraal station—gateway to the city

Damrak street—a buffet of Dutch clichés

historic neighborhood has become the Red Light District (✪ see the Red Light District Walk). Towering above the old part of town is St. Nicholas Church. It was built in the 1880s, when Catholics—after about three centuries of oppression—were finally free to worship in public. To the right of Damrak is the new *(nieuwe)* part of town, where you'll find the Anne Frank House and the peaceful Jordaan neighborhood.

The train station is the city's transportation center. Trams and taxis leave from out front. Beneath your feet is a new Metro line, part of the city's grand infrastructure expansion plans of the "Golden 1990s." Today that investment is paying off, and this plaza, while providing a people-friendly welcome to the city, also works as an efficient transit hub.

On your far right, in front of the Ibis Hotel, is a huge, multistory bikes-only **parking garage.** Biking in Holland is the way to go—the land is flat, distances are short, and there are designated bike paths everywhere. The bike parking garage is completely free, courtesy of the government, and intended to encourage this green and ultra-efficient mode of transportation.

▸ *Let's head out. With your back to the station, start walking south into the city, to the head of Damrak.*

Be careful of trams, bikes, and cars. Keep going south straight along the right side of the street, following the crowds on...

❷ Damrak

This street was once a riverbed. It's where the Amstel River flowed north into the IJ, which led to a vast inlet of the North Sea called the Zuiderzee. It's this unique geography that turned Amsterdam into a center of trade. Boats could sail up the Amstel into the interior of Europe, or out to the North Sea, to reach the rest of the world.

Amsterdam City Walk

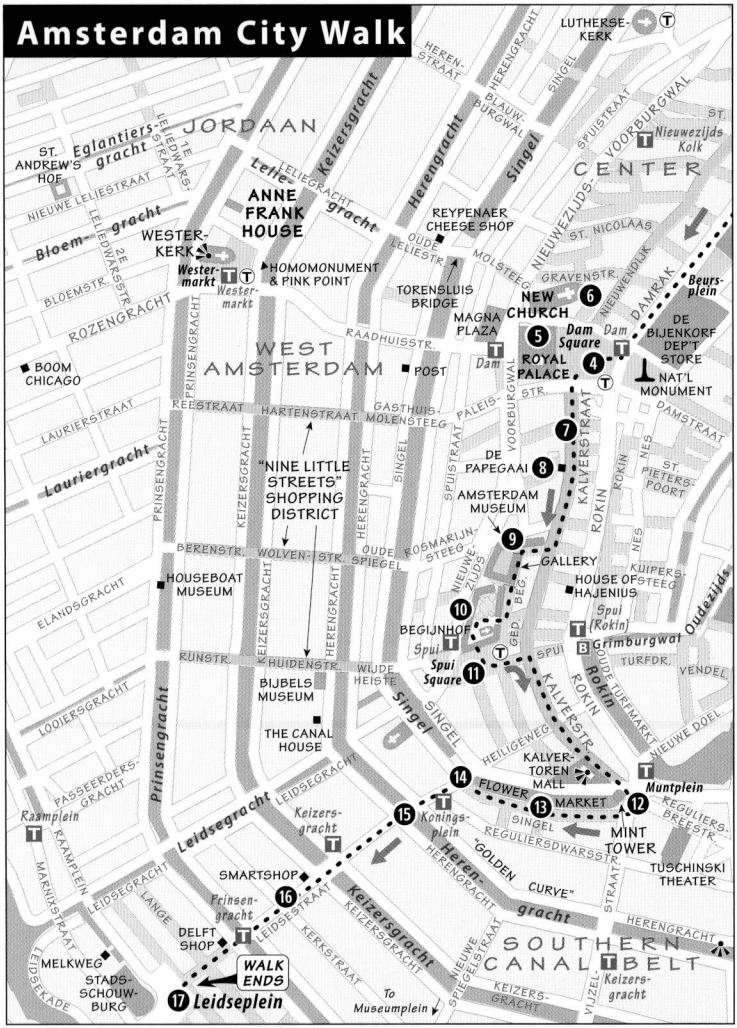
JORDAAN
CENTER
WEST AMSTERDAM
SOUTHERN CANAL BELT
ANNE FRANK HOUSE
WESTER-KERK
Westermarkt
HOMOMONUMENT & PINK POINT
REYPENAER CHEESE SHOP
TORENSLUIS BRIDGE
NEW CHURCH
MAGNA PLAZA
Dam Square
ROYAL PALACE
DE BIJENKORF DEPT STORE
NAT'L MONUMENT
Beursplein
Nieuwezijds Kolk
LUTHERSE-KERK
ST. ANDREW'S HOF
BOOM CHICAGO
POST
"NINE LITTLE STREETS" SHOPPING DISTRICT
DE PAPEGAAI
AMSTERDAM MUSEUM
GALLERY
HOUSE OF HAJENIUS
HOUSEBOAT MUSEUM
BEGIJNHOF
Spui Square
Grimburgwal
BIJBELS MUSEUM
THE CANAL HOUSE
KALVER-TOREN MALL
FLOWER MARKET
Muntplein
MINT TOWER
TUSCHINSKI THEATER
Konings-plein
"GOLDEN CURVE"
Raamplein
SMARTSHOP
DELFT SHOP
MELKWEG
STADS-SCHOUW-BURG
WALK ENDS
Leidseplein
To Museumplein
Eglantiers-gracht
Bloem-gracht
Lelie-gracht
Keizersgracht
Herengracht
Singel
Lauriergracht
Prinsengracht
Leidsegracht
Heiligeweg
Reguliersdwarsstr.
Reguliersbreestr.
Kalverstr.
Rokin
Damrak
Nieuwezijds-voorburgwal
Nieuwezijds-kolk
Oudezijds
Kerkstraat
Leidsestraat
Spiegelstraat
Nieuwe-spiegelstraat
Keizers-gracht
Prinsen-gracht
Raamplein
Marnixstraat
Leidsekade
Passeerders-gracht
Looiersgracht
Elandsgracht
Runstr.
Berenstr.
Wolvenstr.
Huidenstr.
Wijde Heiste
Oude Spiegel
Kosmarijn-steeg
Spuistraat
Reestraat
Hartenstraat
Gasthuis-molensteeg
Raadhuisstr.
Molsteeg
Oude Leliestr.
Nieuwe Leliestraat
Bloemstr.
Rozengracht
Prinsengracht
Keizersgracht
Herengracht
Singel
Voorburgwal
Nieuwezijds-voorburgwal
Blauwburgwal
Herenstraat
Gravenstr.
Nieuwendijk
Damstraat
Dam
Rokin
Kuipers-steeg
Turfdr.
Vendel
Nieuwe Doelen
Spui
Heiligeweg
Singel
Leidsegracht
Keizersgracht
Herengracht
Prinsengracht
Lelie-gracht
Lelie-gracht straat
Eerste Leliewarsstraat
Tweede Leliewarsstr.
Nieuwe Spiegelstraat
Keizersgracht
Vijzel
Keizers-gracht
Herengracht
Straat
Herengracht
Singel
Heren-straat
Lutherse-kerk
Nieuwezijds Kolk
St.
Voorburgwal
Spuistraat
Nieuwendijk
Damrak
Nieuwezijds-voorburgwal
St. Nicolaas
Gravenstr.
Molsteeg
Oude Leliestr.
Leliegracht
Bloemstr.
Rozengracht
Prinsengracht
Reestraat
Hartenstraat
Gasthuis-molensteeg
Raadhuisstr.
Dam
Voorburgwal
Paleis-str.
Spuistraat
Kalverstraat
Rokin
Damstraat
Nes
St. Pieters-poort
Kosmarijn-steeg
Berenstr.
Wolvenstr.
Oude Spiegel
Nieuwe-zijds
Ged. Beg.
Kuipers-steeg
Spui
Grimburgwal
Turfdr.
Vendel
Nieuwe Doelen
Heiligeweg
Singel
Leidsegracht
Keizersgracht
Herengracht
Prinseng

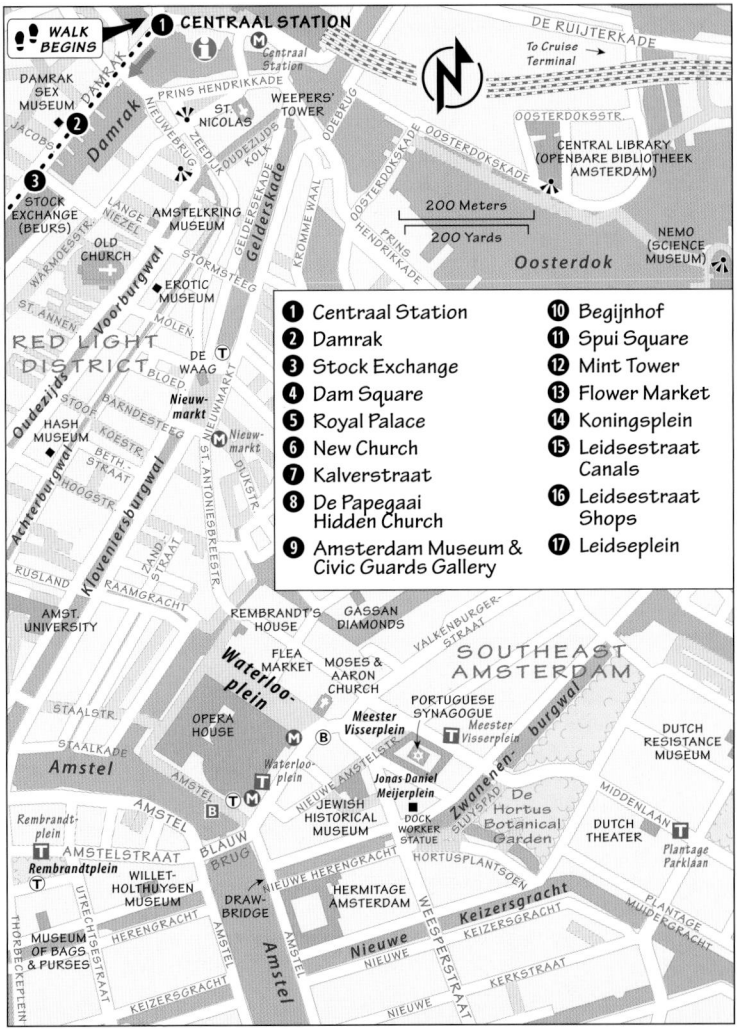
WALK BEGINS
1 CENTRAAL STATION
Centraal Station
DE RUIJTERKADE
To Cruise Terminal
DAMRAK SEX MUSEUM
2
Damrak
PRINS HENDRIKKADE
ST. NICOLAS
WEEPERS' TOWER
JACOBS
NIEUWEBRUG
ZEEDIJK
OUDEZIJDS KOLK
ODEBRUG
OOSTERDOKSSTR.
OOSTERDOKSKADE
CENTRAL LIBRARY (OPENBARE BIBLIOTHEEK AMSTERDAM)
3
STOCK EXCHANGE (BEURS)
LANGE NIEZEL
AMSTELKRING MUSEUM
GELDERSEKADE
Gelderskade
KROMME WAAL
200 Meters
200 Yards
NEMO (SCIENCE MUSEUM)
Oosterdok
WARMOESSTR.
OLD CHURCH
Voorburgwal
STORMSTEEG
EROTIC MUSEUM
ST. ANNEN
MOLEN
RED LIGHT DISTRICT
DE WAAG
BLOED
Nieuwmarkt
Oudezijds
STOOF
BARNDESTEEG
HASH MUSEUM
KOESTR.
BETH-STRAAT
Nieuwmarkt
NIEUWMARKT
ST. ANTONIESBREESTR.
DIJKSTR.
Achterburgwal
HOOGSTR.
Kloveniersburgwal
ZAND-STRAAT
RUSLAND
RAAMGRACHT
AMST. UNIVERSITY
REMBRANDT'S HOUSE
GASSAN DIAMONDS
VALKENBURGER-STRAAT
SOUTHEAST AMSTERDAM
FLEA MARKET
MOSES & AARON CHURCH
Waterloo-plein
STAALSTR.
OPERA HOUSE
Meester Visserplein
PORTUGUESE SYNAGOGUE
Meester Visserplein
Zwanenburgwal
DUTCH RESISTANCE MUSEUM
STAALKADE
Amstel
Waterloo-plein
NIEUWE AMSTELSTR.
Jonas Daniel Meijerplein
AMSTEL
JEWISH HISTORICAL MUSEUM
DOCK WORKER STATUE
SLUYSPAD
De Hortus Botanical Garden
MIDDENLAAN
DUTCH THEATER
Plantage Parklaan
Rembrandt-plein
AMSTELSTRAAT
Rembrandtplein
BLAUW BRUG
NIEUWE HERENGRACHT
HORTUSPLANTSOEN
WILLET-HOLTHUYSEN MUSEUM
DRAW-BRIDGE
HERMITAGE AMSTERDAM
WEESPERSTRAAT
Keizersgracht
KEIZERSGRACHT
PLANTAGE MUIDERGRACHT
UTRECHTSESTRAAT
HERENGRACHT
THORBECKEPLEIN
MUSEUM OF BAGS & PURSES
Amstel
Nieuwe
NIEUWE
KERKSTRAAT
KEIZERSGRACHT
1 Centraal Station
2 Damrak
3 Stock Exchange
4 Dam Square
5 Royal Palace
6 New Church
7 Kalverstraat
8 De Papegaai Hidden Church
9 Amsterdam Museum & Civic Guards Gallery
10 Begijnhof
11 Spui Square
12 Mint Tower
13 Flower Market
14 Koningsplein
15 Leidsestraat Canals
16 Leidsestraat Shops
17 Leidseplein

As you stroll along Damrak, look left. There's a marina, lined with old brick buildings. Though they aren't terribly historic, the scene still captures a bit of Golden Age Amsterdam. Think of it: Back in the 1600s, this area was the harbor, and those buildings warehoused exotic goods from all over the world.

All along Damrak, you'll pass a veritable gauntlet of touristy shops. These seem to cover every Dutch cliché. You'll see wooden shoes, which the Dutch used to wear to get around easily in the marshy soil, and all manner of tulips; the real ones come from Holland's famed fresh-flower industry. Heineken fridge magnets advertise one of the world's most popular pilsner beers. There are wheels of cheese, marijuana-leaf hats, team jerseys for the Ajax football (soccer) club, and memorabilia with the city's "XXX" logo. You'll likely hear a hand-cranked barrel organ and see windmill-shaped saltshakers. And everything seems to be available in bright orange—the official color of the Dutch royal family.

At the **Damrak Sex Museum** (Damrak 18; see page 120), you'll find the city's most notorious commodity on display. As a port town catering to sailors and businessmen away from home, Amsterdam has always accommodated the sex trade. Continue up Damrak for more touristy delectables: Teasers (at #36) is the local Hooters. French fry stands advertise the popular local fast food as *Vlaamse friets*—Flemish fries—since they were invented in the Low Countries. The stand at Damrak 41 is a favorite, where locals stop to dip their fries in mayonnaise (not ketchup).

Many of Damrak's eateries are ethnic. Here, international cuisine is almost like going local. Restaurants serving *rijsttafel,* a sampler of assorted Indonesian dishes, are especially popular, thanks to the days when the Dutch East Indies were a colony. Amsterdammers on the go usually just grab a simple sandwich *(broodje)* or a pita-bread wrap *(shoarma)* from a Middle Eastern takeout joint.

We're walking along what was once the Amstel River. Today, the Amstel is channeled into canals and its former mouth is covered by Centraal station. But Amsterdam still remains a major seaport. That's because, in the 19th century, the Dutch dug the North Sea Canal to create a shorter route to the open sea. These days, more than 100,000 ships a year dock on the outskirts of Amsterdam, making it Europe's fourth-busiest seaport (giant cruise ships stop here as well). For all of Amsterdam's existence, it's been a trading center.

▸ *The long brick building with the square clock tower, along the left side of Damrak, is the...*

❸ Stock Exchange (Beurs van Berlage)

This impressive structure, a symbol of the city's long tradition as a trading town, was built with nine million bricks. Like so many buildings in this once-marshy city, it was constructed on a foundation of pilings—some 5,000 tree trunks hammered vertically into the soil. When the Beurs opened in 1903, it was one of the world's first modernist buildings, with a geometric, minimal, no-frills style. Emphasizing function over looks, it helped set the architectural tone for many 20th-century buildings.

Make your way to the end of the long, century-old building. Amsterdammers have gathered in this neighborhood to trade since medieval times. Back then, "trading stock" meant buying and selling goats, chickens, or kegs of beer. Over time, they began exchanging slips of paper, or "futures," rather than actual goods. Traders needed moneychangers, who needed bankers, who made money by lending money. By the 1600s, Amsterdam had become one of the world's first great capitalist cities, loaning money to free-spending kings, dukes, and bishops.

When you reach the end of the building, detour left into the square called **Beursplein.** In 1984, the Beurs building was turned into a cultural center, and the stock exchange moved next door to the Euronext complex. Amsterdam still thrives as the center of Dutch business and, besides Heineken, is home to Shell Oil and Philips Electronics.

▸ *Continue along Damrak until it opens into Dam Square. Make your way—carefully—across the street to the cobblestone pavement. Now, stand in the middle of the square and take it all in.*

❹ Dam Square

This is the historic heart of Amsterdam. Around the year 1250, some local fishermen built a *damme,* blocking the Amstel River and creating a small village called "Amstel-damme." To the north was the *damrak* (meaning "outer harbor"), a waterway that eventually led to the sea. To the south was the *rokin* ("inner harbor"), for river traffic. With access to the sea, fishermen were soon trading with German riverboats traveling downstream and with seafaring boats from Stockholm, Hamburg, and London. Dam Square was the center of it all.

Today, Dam Square is still the center of Dutch life, at least symbolically.

Amsterdam's Story

Visualize the physical layout of this man-made city: built on trees, protected by dikes, and laced with canals in the marshy delta at the mouth of the Amstel River. Location, location, location. Boats could arrive here from Germany by riverboat down the Rhine, from England across the Channel and down the IJ, and from Denmark by entering the Zuiderzee inlet of the North Sea. No wonder that St. Nicholas, protector of water travelers, was the city's patron saint.

As early as 1300, Amsterdam was already an international trade center for German beer, locally caught herring, cloth, bacon, salt, and wine. Having dammed and canalized the Amstel and diked out the sea tides, the Dutch drained land, sunk pilings, and built a city from scratch. When the region's leading bishop granted the town a charter (1300), Amsterdammers could then set up law courts, judge their own matters, and be essentially autonomous. The town thrived.

By 1500, Amsterdam was a walled city of 12,000, with the Singel canal serving as the moat. The city had a midcentury growth spurt when its trading rival Antwerp fell to Spanish troops, and a flood of fellow Flemish headed north, fleeing chaos and religious persecution.

In 1602, hardy Dutch sailors (and Henry Hudson, an Englishman in Dutch service) tried their hand at trade with the Far East. When they returned, they brought with them valuable spices, jewels, luxury goods...and the Golden Age.

The Dutch East India Company (abbreviated as "VOC" in Dutch), a state-subsidized import/export business, combined nautical skills with capitalist investing. With 500 or so 150-foot ships cruising in and out of Amsterdam's harbor, it was the first great multinational corporation. Amsterdam's Golden Age (c. 1600-1650) rode the wave of hard work and good fortune. Over the next two centuries, the VOC broadened the horizons of a half-million Dutch people, sending them on business trips to Asia.

This city of the Golden Age was perhaps the wealthiest on earth, thriving as the "warehouse of the world." Goods came from

everywhere. The VOC's specialties were spices (pepper and cinnamon), coffee and tea, Chinese porcelain (Delftware's Eastern inspiration), and silk. Meanwhile, the competing Dutch West India Company concentrated on the New World, trading African slaves for South American sugar. With its wealth, Amsterdam built in grand style, erecting the gabled townhouses we see today. The city expanded west and south, adding new neighborhoods.

But by 1650, Amsterdam's overseas trade began to be eclipsed by new superpowers—England and France. Inconclusive wars with Louis XIV and England drained the economy, destroyed the trading fleet, and demoralized the people. Throughout the 1700s, Amsterdam was a city of backwater bankers rather than international traders, although it remained the cultural center of Holland. In early 1795, Napoleon's French troops occupied the country, and the economy was dismal.

Technological achievements spurred a revival in the 1800s. The Dutch built a canal reconnecting Amsterdam directly with the North Sea (1824-1876), railroads laced the small country, and the city expanded southward by draining new land. The Rijksmuseum, Centraal train station, and main post office (now the Magna Plaza shopping center) were built as proud monuments to the economic upswing.

The 1930s Depression hit hard, followed by five years of occupation under the Nazis, aided by pro-Nazi Dutch. The city's large Jewish population was decimated by Nazi deportations and extermination (falling from about 75,000 Jews in 1940 to just 15,000 in 1945).

With postwar prosperity, 1960s Amsterdam again became a world cultural capital as the center for Europe's hippies, who came here to smoke marijuana. Grassroots campaigns by young, artistic, politically active people promoted free sex and free bikes.

Today, Amsterdam is a city of 820,000 people jammed into small apartments (often with the same floor plan as their neighbors'). Since the 1970s, many immigrants have become locals. One in 10 Amsterdammers is Surinamese, and one in 10 prays toward Mecca.

Dam Square, with its World War II memorial, is the symbolic center of the Netherlands.

The Royal Palace and major department stores face the square. Mimes, jugglers, and human statues mingle with locals and tourists. As Holland's most recognizable place, Dam Square is where political demonstrations begin and end.

Circling the Square: Pan the square clockwise, and take in the sights, starting with the Royal Palace—the large domed building on the west side. To its right stands the New Church (Nieuwe Kerk). Panning past Damrak, see the proud old De Bijenkorf ("The Beehive") department store (with a nice-view café).

Farther right, the Grand Hotel Krasnapolsky has a lovely circa-1900 glass-roofed "winter garden." The white obelisk is the National Monument, honoring WWII casualties. A few blocks behind the hotel is the edge of the Red Light District. To the right of the hotel stretches the street called the Nes, lined with some of Amsterdam's edgy live-theater venues. Panning farther right, find Rokin street—Damrak's southern counterpart. Next, just to the right of the touristy Madame Tussauds, is Kalverstraat, a busy pedestrian-only shoppers mall.

City on a Sandbar

Amsterdam sits in the marshy delta at the mouth of the Amstel River—a completely man-made city, built on millions of wooden pilings. (The wood survives if kept wet and out of the air.) Since World War II, concrete has been used for the pilings, with foundations as deep as 120 feet.

In the Middle Ages, buildings were made of wood. But after a series of devastating fires, brick became the building material of choice. Many of the city's old buildings lean this way and that as their pilings settle.

❺ Royal Palace (Koninklijk Huis)

Despite the name, this is really the former City Hall—and Amsterdam is one of the cradles of modern democracy. In medieval times, this was where the city council and mayor met. Amsterdam was a self-governing community that prided itself on its independence and thumbed its nose at royalty. In about 1650, the old medieval Town Hall was replaced with this one. Its style is appropriately Classical, recalling the democratic Greeks. The triangular pediment features denizens of the sea cavorting with Neptune and his gilded copper trident—all appropriate imagery for sea-trading Amsterdam. The small balcony (just above the entry doors) is where city leaders have long appeared for major speeches, pronouncements, executions, and (these days) for newly married royalty to blow kisses to the crowds.

Today, the palace remains one of the four official residences of King Willem-Alexander and is usually open to visitors (see page 116).

▸ *A few paces away, to the right as you're facing the Royal Palace, is the...*

❻ New Church (Nieuwe Kerk)

Though called the "New" Church, this building is actually 600 years old—a mere 100 years newer than the "Old" Church (in the Red Light District). The sundial above the entrance once served as the city's official timepiece.

While it's pricey to enter the church, cheapskates can see much of it for free. Enter the gift shop (through the "Museumshop" door to the left of the main entrance), and climb the stairs to a balcony with a small free museum and great views of the nave.

The church's bare, spacious, well-lit interior (occupied by a new

Royal Palace on Dam Square

New Church, where monarchs are crowned

art exhibit every three months) looks quite different from the Baroque-encrusted churches found in the rest of Europe. In 1566, clear-eyed Protestant extremists throughout Holland marched into Catholic churches (including this one), lopped off the heads of holy statues, stripped gold-leaf angels from the walls, urinated on Virgin Marys, and shattered stained-glass windows in a wave of anti-Catholic vandalism.

This iconoclasm (icon-breaking) of 1566 started an 80-year war against Spain and the Habsburgs, leading finally to Dutch independence in 1648. Catholic churches like this one were converted to the new dominant religion, Calvinist Protestantism (today's Dutch Reformed Church). From then on, Dutch churches downplayed the "graven images" and "idols" of ornate religious art.

Take in the church's main highlights. At the far left end is an organ from 1655, still played for midday concerts. Opposite the entrance, a stained-glass window shows Count William IV giving the city its "XXX" coat of arms. The window over the entrance portrays the inauguration of Queen Wilhelmina (1880-1962), who became the steadfast center of the Dutch resistance during World War II. The choir, once used by the monks, was, after the Reformation, turned into a mausoleum for a great Dutch admiral.

This church is where many of the Netherlands' monarchs are married, and all are "inaugurated." (Dutch royals never actually wear the official crown.) In April 2013, King Willem-Alexander—Wilhelmina's great-grandson—paraded through this church to the golden choir screen, where he was presented with the royal crown, scepter, orb, sword, and a copy of the Dutch constitution. With TV lights glaring and cameras flashing, he was sworn in as the new sovereign.

Back outside, look at the **monument** standing tall in the middle of

Dam Square. This white obelisk was built in 1956 as a WWII memorial. The Nazis occupied Holland from 1940 to 1945; in those years they deported some 60,000 Jewish Amsterdammers, driving many, including young Anne Frank and her family—into hiding. Near the end of the war, the "Hunger Winter" of 1944-1945 killed thousands of Dutch and forced many to survive on little more than tulip bulbs. The national monument—with its carvings of the crucified Christ, men in chains, and howling dogs—remembers the suffering of that grim time. Now the structure is also considered a monument for peace.

▸ *From Dam Square, head south (at the* Rabobank *sign) on...*

❼ Kalverstraat

Kalverstraat (strictly pedestrian-only—even bikers need to dismount and walk) has been a traditional shopping street for centuries. But today it's notorious among locals as a noisy, soulless string of chain stores. For smaller and more elegant stores, try the adjacent district called De Negen Straatjes ("The Nine Little Streets"). Only about four blocks west of Kalverstraat, it's where 200 or so shops and cafés mingle along tranquil canals.

▸ *About 100 yards along, keep a sharp eye out for the next sight (it's fairly easy to miss): on the right, just before and across from the McDonald's, at #58. Now pop into...*

❽ De Papegaai Hidden Church (Petrus en Paulus Kerk)

This Catholic church is an oasis of peace amid crass 21st-century commercialism. It's not exactly a hidden church (after all, you've found it), but it still keeps a low profile. That's because it dates from an era when Catholics in Amsterdam were forced to worship in secret.

In the 1500s, as Protestants were fighting Catholics all over Europe, Amsterdam was taken over by Protestant extremists. For the next two centuries, Catholic worship was illegal, though it was tolerated so long as it was practiced in humble, unadvertised places, like this church.

▸ *Continue south on Kalverstraat for about 100 yards. At #92, where Kalverstraat crosses Wijde Kapel Steeg, turn right to enter the complex housing the...*

❾ Amsterdam Museum and Civic Guards Gallery

Pause at the entrance to the museum complex to view the archway with Amsterdam's coat of arms. The X-shaped crosses on the red shield

represent (not the sex trade, but...) the crucifixion of St. Andrew, the patron saint of fishermen. The crown is the Habsburg royal crown, granted to Amsterdam as thanks for a loan from Dutch bankers.

Continue under the arch, past a pleasant café, a shaded courtyard, and lockers from the old orphanage. Up ahead is the **Amsterdam Museum** (described on page 118).

Next to the museum's entrance is a free, glassed-in passageway lined with paintings. If it's closed, you'll need to backtrack to Kalverstraat to continue our walk (continue south, then turn right on Begijnensteeg, then look for the gate leading to the Begijnhof). Otherwise, step into the **Civic Guards Gallery** (Schuttersgalerij).

This hall features group portraits of Amsterdam's citizens from the Golden Age to modern times. Giant statues of Goliath and a knee-high David (from 1650) watch over the whole thing.

Stroll around and gaze into the eyes of the hardworking men and women who made tiny Holland so prosperous and powerful. These are ordinary middle-class people, merchants, and traders, dressed in their Sunday best. They come across as good people—honest, businesslike, and friendly.

The Dutch got rich the old-fashioned way—they earned it. By 1600, Holland's merchant fleets commanded the seas. Traders, who were financed by shrewd Amsterdam businessmen, flourished by shipping goods from Dutch colonies as far away as India, the East Indies, and America.

The portraits show proud men gathered with their Civic Guard militia units. These men defended Holland, but the Civic Guards were also fraternal organizations of business bigwigs—the Rotary Clubs of the 17th century. The weapons they carry—pikes and muskets—are mostly symbolic.

The Amsterdam Museum's entrance arch

Civic Guard group portrait—"Say *kaas*."

Many paintings look the same in this highly stylized genre. The men usually sit arranged in two rows. Someone holds the militia's flag. Later group portraits showed "captains" of industry going about their work, dressed in suits, along with the tools of their trade—ledger books, quill pens, and money.

Everyone looks straight out, and every face is lit perfectly. Each paid for his own portrait and wanted it right. It took masters like Rembrandt and Frans Hals to take the starch out of the collars and compose more natural scenes.

Now focus on some more modern portraits. The collection rotates. You may see simple photos of today's ordinary citizens—workers, police—the backbone of this democracy, or the modern-day town council posing as Golden Age bigwigs.

▸ *Exit out the far end of the Civic Guards Gallery. Once in the light of day, continue ahead one block farther south and find the humble gate on the right, which leads to the...*

⑩ Begijnhof

This quiet courtyard, lined with houses around a church, has sheltered women since 1346. This was the home of a community of Beguines—pious and simple women who removed themselves from the world at large to dedicate their lives to God.

As you enter, keep in mind that this spot isn't just a tourist attraction; it's also a place where people live. Be considerate: Don't photograph the residents or their homes, be quiet, and stick to the area near the churches.

Just beyond the church you'll find a **statue** of one of these charitable sisters. The Beguines' ranks swelled during the Golden Age, when so many women were widowed by the hazards of overseas trade. Poor and rich women alike turned their backs on materialism and marriage to live here in Christian poverty, serving others. Though obedient to a mother superior, the members of the lay order of Beguines were not nuns. They spent their days deep in prayer, spinning wool, making lace, teaching, and caring for the sick.

Now turn your attention to the brick-faced **English Reformed church** (Engelse Kerk), built in 1420 to serve the Beguine community. In 1607, the church became Anglican. The church served as a refuge for English traders and religious separatists fleeing persecution in England. Strict Protestants such as the famous Pilgrims found sanctuary in tolerant

Begijnhof—quiet courtyard for lay sisters

Beautiful interior of the "hidden" Catholic church

Amsterdam, worshipping in this church before sailing to religious freedom in America. If the church is open, step inside and head to the far end, toward the stained-glass window. It shows the Pilgrims praying before boarding the Mayflower. Along the right-hand wall is an old pew they may have sat on, and on the altar is a Bible from 1763, with lotſ of old-ſtyle ſ's. Also of note is the front pulpit, carved of wood. It's by Piet Mondrian, the famous Dutch abstract artist, and was one of his first professional gigs.

Back outside, find the **Catholic church,** which faces the English Reformed Church. Because Catholics were being persecuted when it was built, this had to be a low-profile, "hidden" church—notice the painted-out windows on the second and third floors. Step inside, through the low-profile doorway. It's decorated lovingly, if on the cheap (try tapping softly on a "marble" column). Amsterdam's Catholics must have eagerly awaited the day when they were legally allowed to say Mass (that day finally came in the 19th century).

Today, Holland still has something of a religious divide, but not a bitter one. Amsterdam itself is pretty un-churched. But the Dutch countryside is much more religious, including a "Bible Belt" region where 98 percent of the population is Protestant. Overall, in the Netherlands, the country is divided fairly evenly between Catholics, Protestants, and those who see Sunday as a day to sleep in and enjoy a lazy brunch.

Step back outside. The last Beguine died in 1971, but this Begijnhof still provides subsidized housing to about 100 single women (mostly Catholic seniors). The Begijnhof is just one of a few dozen *hofjes* (little housing projects surrounding courtyards) that dot Amsterdam.

The statue of the Beguine faces a black **wooden house** (at #34), the city's oldest, from 1528. Originally, the whole city consisted of wooden

houses like this one. They were eventually replaced with brick houses, to minimize the fire danger.

▸ *Near the wooden house, find a little corridor leading you back into the modern world. Head up a few steps to emerge into the lively...*

⓫ Spui Square

Lined with cafés and bars, this square is one of the city's more popular spots for nightlife and sunny afternoon people-watching. Its name, Spui (rhymes with "now" and means "spew"), recalls the days when water was moved over dikes to keep the place dry.

Head two blocks to the left, crossing busy Kalverstraat, to the street called the Rokin. Turn left and walk up 50 yards to a mecca for cigar connoisseurs—the House of Hajenius cigar store, at Rokin 92. Enter this sumptuous Art Deco building with painted leather ceilings. Don't be shy—the place is as much a free museum for visitors as it is a store for paying customers.

From Hajenius, backtrack to Kalverstraat and head south. Just before the end of this shopping boulevard, on the right, you'll see modern **Kalvertoren** shopping mall. Inside, the slanting glass elevator takes people to the top floor to enjoy something that's rare in altitude-challenged Amsterdam—a nice view.

▸ *At the center of the square stands the...*

⓬ Mint Tower (Munttoren)

The tower marked the limit of the medieval walled city and served as one of its original gates. In the Middle Ages, the city walls were girdled by a moat—the Singel canal. Until about 1500, the area beyond here was nothing but marshy fields and a few farms on reclaimed land. The Mint Tower's steeple was added later—in the year 1620, as you can see written below the clock face.

Today, the tower is a favorite within Amsterdam's marijuana culture. Stoners love to take a photo of the clock and its 1620 sign at exactly 4:20 p.m.—the traditional time to quit work and light one up. (On the 24-hour clock, 4:20 p.m. is 16:20...Du-u-u-ude!)

▸ *Continue past the Mint Tower, first walking a few yards south along busy Vijzelstraat (keep an eye out for trams). Then turn right and walk west along the south bank of the Singel canal. It's lined with the greenhouse shops of the...*

The Mint Tower once marked the border of the medieval, walled city.

"Tulip mania" lives on at the Flower Market.

Be daring—try a herring.

⓭ Flower Market (Bloemenmarkt)

The stands along this busy block sell cut flowers, plants, bulbs, seeds, garden supplies, and flower-oriented souvenirs and knickknacks. Browse your way toward the end of the block.

The Flower Market is a testament to Holland's long-time love affair with flowers. The Netherlands is by far the largest flower exporter in Europe, and a major flower power worldwide. If you're looking for a souvenir, note that certain seeds are marked as OK to bring back through customs into the US (the marijuana starter-kit-in-a-can is probably...not).

The best-known Dutch flower, the tulip, was brought from central Asia in the mid-1500s. The hardy bulbs thrived in the sandy soil of Holland's reclaimed land. Within a generation, tulips grew from a trendy fad into an all-out frenzy. Soon, a single prized bulb could sell for the equivalent of thousands of dollars. By 1637, it was full-blown "Tulip mania"—yes, that's what even the Dutch called it. Then the tulip bubble burst. Overnight, once-wealthy investors were broke. The crash was devastating, even playing a role in the decline of the Golden Age. But Holland's love of this delightful flower lived on. Today, tulips are a major export, and are firmly planted in the Dutch psyche.

▸ *The long Flower Market ends at the next bridge, where you'll see a square named...*

⓮ Koningsplein

Here there's a popular herring shop. The sign *Hollandse nieuwe* means the herring are "new" (fresh), caught during the May-June season. Amsterdammers like to eat the fish chopped up with onions and pickles, using the Dutch-flag toothpick as a utensil. Elsewhere in the Netherlands,

Leidsestraat—busy with trams and shoppers

Delftware—blue-painted ceramics

people are more likely to eat the fish whole—you grab it by the tail, tip your head back, and down she goes.

▸ *Turn left, heading straight south to Leidseplein along Koningsplein, which changes its name to Leidsestraat.*

⓯ Leidsestraat Canals and ⓰ Shops

The first of several grand canals you'll pass is Herengracht.

Look left down Herengracht to see the so-called **Golden Curve** of the canal. It's lined with townhouses sporting especially nice gables. Amsterdam has many different types of gable—bell-shaped, step-shaped, and so on. This stretch is best known for its "cornice" gables (straight across). These topped the Classical-looking facades belonging to rich merchants—the *heren.* (For more on gables, see the sidebar on page 91.)

There are so many canals in Amsterdam because the city was founded in a marshy river delta, so they needed to keep the water at bay. They dammed the Amstel River and channeled it safely away into canals, creating pockets of dry land to build on.

The word *gracht* (pronounced, roughly, "hroht," with guttural flair) can refer to a canal itself, or to the ensemble of a canal and the lanes that border it on each side. Today, the city has about 100 canals, most of which are about 10 feet deep. They're crossed by some 1,200 bridges, fringed with 100,000 Dutch elm and lime trees, and bedecked with 2,500 houseboats. A system of locks (back near the Centraal station) controls the flow. The locks are opened periodically to flush out the system.

Leidsestraat is a busy street, crowded with shoppers, tourists, bicycles, and trams (keep your wits about you along here, and don't walk on

the tram tracks). Notice that, as the street narrows, trams must wait their turn to share a single track.

Cross over the next canal (Keizersgracht) and find the little **smartshop** on the right-hand corner (at Kaisersgracht 508). "Smartshops" like this one are fully licensed businesses that sell drugs—some of them quite strong, most of them illegal back home, and not all of them harmless. But since all these products are found in nature, the Dutch government considers them legal. (For more on smartshops, see page 71.) You can check out the window displays, or go on in and browse.

Just over the next bridge, where Leidsestraat crosses Prinsengracht, you'll find the **Delft Blue Shop** (to the right, at Prinsengracht 440). This place sells good examples of the glazed ceramics known as Delftware, famous for its distinctive blue-and-white designs. In the 1600s, Dutch traders brought home blue-and-white porcelain from China, which became so popular that Dutch potters scrambled to come up with their own version. It was traditionally made in Delft, the quaint town about 30 miles southwest of here. You might spot a tulip vase in the window: a tall, tapering "flower pagoda" with multiple spouts for displaying the prized flower.

▸ *Follow Leidsestraat down to the big, busy square, called...*

⓱ Leidseplein

This is Amsterdam's liveliest square: filled with outdoor tables under trees; ringed with cafés, theaters, and nightclubs; bustling with tourists, diners, trams, mimes, and fire eaters. No wonder locals and tourists alike come here day and night to sit under the trees and sip a coffee or beer in the warmth of the sun or the glow of lantern light.

Do a 360-degree spin: Leidseplein's south side is bordered by a gray Neoclassical building that houses a huge Apple Store—sitting on what may be the city's most expensive piece of real estate. Nearby is the city's main serious theater, the **Stadsschouwburg.**

To the right of the Stadsschouwburg is a lane leading to the **Melkweg** ("Milky Way") nightclub. Back in the 1970s, this place was almost mythical—an entertainment complex entirely devoted to the young generation and their desires.

Continue panning. The neighborhood beyond Burger King is Amsterdam's **"Restaurant Row,"** featuring Thai, Brazilian, Indian, Italian, Indonesian—and even a few Dutch—eateries.

Next, on the east end of Leidseplein, is the flagship **Bulldog Café**

The Bulldog Café coffeeshop on Leidseplein, a place to kick back after this walk.

and Coffeeshop. (Notice the sign above the door: It once housed the police bureau.) A small green-and-white decal on the window indicates that it's a city-licensed "coffeeshop," where marijuana is sold and smoked legally. Incredible as that may seem to visitors from the States, it's been going on here in Amsterdam for nearly four decades—another Dutch cliché alongside windmill peppermills and wooden shoes.

▸ *Our walk is over. But those with more energy could get out their maps and make their way to Vondelpark or the Rijksmuseum. To return to Centraal station (or to nearly anyplace along this walk), catch tram #1, #2, or #5 from Leidseplein.*

Rijksmuseum Tour

At Amsterdam's Rijksmuseum ("Rijks" rhymes with "bikes"), Holland's Golden Age shines with the best collection anywhere of the Dutch Masters—from Vermeer's quiet domestic scenes and Steen's raucous family meals to Hals' snapshot portraits and Rembrandt's moody brilliance.

The 17th century saw the Netherlands at the pinnacle of its power. Trade and shipping boomed, wealth poured in, and the arts flourished. Upper-middle-class businessmen hired artists to paint their portraits and decorate their homes with pretty still lifes and unpreachy, slice-of-life art.

Dutch art is meant to be enjoyed, not studied. It's straightforward, meat-and-potatoes art for the common man. On this visit, we'll enjoy the beauty of everyday things rendered in exquisite detail. Set your cerebral cortex on "low" and let this art pass straight from the eyes to the heart, with minimal detours.

ORIENTATION

Cost: €17.50.

Hours: Daily 9:00-17:00.

Advance Tickets: If you buy tickets online at www.rijksmuseum.nl, you can enter the building through a special (less-crowded) entrance. The ticket is good any time (no entry time specified).

Avoiding Crowds/Lines: The museum is most crowded on weekends and holidays, and between 11:00 and 14:00. It's least crowded after 15:00.

Getting There: From Centraal station, catch tram #2 or #5 to the Rijksmuseum stop. The museum entrance is inside the arched passage that cuts through the building at its center.

Information: The helpful info desk in the lower-level Atrium has free maps and baggage check. Info tel. 020/674-7047, www.rijksmuseum.nl.

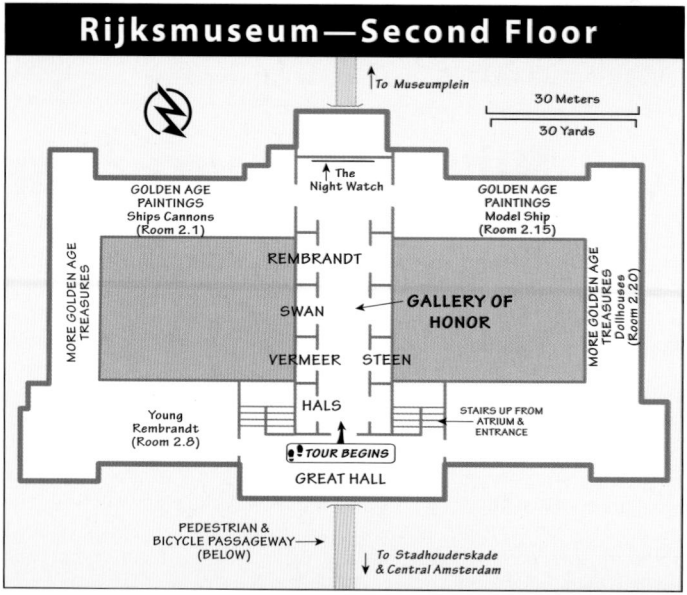

Tours: Guided tours are often offered at 11:00, 13:00, and 15:00 (€5). A multimedia videoguide (€5) offers both a 45-minute highlights tour and a more in-depth tour. Use this chapter to hit the highlights, then (if you choose) explore the rest of the collection with the videoguide.

Length of This Tour: Allow 1.5 hours.

Photography: Permitted but no flash.

Cuisine Art: The Rijksmuseum Grand Café is in the Atrium. (No museum ticket required to eat here.) Beyond the museum complex, you'll find the Cobra Café on Museumplein. Vondelpark and Museumplein are perfect for picnics.

Starring: Rembrandt van Rijn, Frans Hals, Johannes Vermeer, Jan Steen.

THE TOUR BEGINS

▸ *From the lower level Atrium, show your ticket and follow the crowds up the stairway to the top (second) floor, arriving at the Great Hall. With its stained-glass windows, vaulted ceiling, and murals of Golden Age explorers, this place feels like a cathedral to Holland's middle-class merchants. Now, follow the flow into the...*

Gallery of Honor

This grand space was purpose-built to hold the Greatest Hits of the Golden Age by the era's biggest rock stars: Hals, Vermeer, Steen, and Rembrandt. The best of the era's portraits, still lifes, landscapes, and slice-of-life "genre scenes" give us a close-up look at daily life in this happy, affluent era.

The Rijksmuseum, on pleasant Museumplein

The Atrium has tourist services.

Frans Hals

Frans Hals (c. 1582-1666) was the premier Golden Age portrait painter. Merchants hired him the way we'd hire a wedding photographer. With a few quick strokes, Hals captured not only the features, but also the personality.

***A Militiaman Holding a Berkemeyer*, a.k.a. *The Merry Drinker*, c. 1628-1630**

You're greeted by a jovial man in a black hat (see photo on page 35), capturing the earthy, exuberant spirit of the Dutch Golden Age. Notice the details—the happy red face of the man offering us a *berkemeyer* drinking glass, the sparkle in his eyes, the lacy collar, the decorative belt buckle, and so on.

Now move in closer. All these meticulous details are accomplished with a few thick, messy brushstrokes. The beard is a tangle of brown worms, the belt buckle a yellow blur. His hand is a study in smudges. Even the expressive face is created with a few well-chosen patches of color. Unlike Dutch still-life scenes, this canvas is meant to be viewed from a distance, where the colors and brushstrokes blend together.

Rather than posing his subject, making him stand for hours saying "cheese," Hals tried to catch him at a candid moment. He often painted common people, fishermen, and barflies such as this one. He had to work quickly to capture the serendipity of the moment. Hals used a stop-action technique, freezing the man in mid-gesture, with the rough brushwork creating a blur that suggests the man is still moving.

Two centuries later, the Impressionists learned from Hals' scruffy brushwork. In the Van Gogh Museum, you'll see how Van Gogh painted, say, a brown beard by using thick dabs of green, yellow, and red that blend at a distance to make brown.

***Portrait of a Couple, Probably Isaac Abrahamsz Massa and Beatrix van der Laen*, c. 1622**

This likely wedding portrait of a chubby, pleasant merchant and his bride sums up the story of the Dutch Golden Age. Because this overseas trader was away from home for years at a time on business, Hals makes a special effort to point out his patron's commitment to marriage. Isaac pledges allegiance to his wife, putting his hand on his heart. Beatrix's wedding ring is prominently displayed dead center between them (on her right-hand forefinger, Protestant-style). The vine clinging to a tree is a symbol of man's support and woman's dependence. And in the distance at right, in the

The Dutch Golden Age (1600s)

Who bought this art? Look around at the Rijksmuseum's many portraits, and you'll see ordinary middle-class people, merchants, and traders. Even in their Sunday best, you can tell that these are hardworking, businesslike, friendly, simple people (with a penchant for wearing ruffled lace collars).

By 1600, Holland's merchant fleets ruled the waves with colonies as far away as India, the East Indies, and America (remember—New York was originally "Nieuw Amsterdam"). Back home, these traders were financed by shrewd Amsterdam businessmen on the new frontiers of capitalism.

Look around again. Is there even one crucifixion? One saint? One Madonna? In most countries, Catholic bishops and rich kings supported the arts. But the Dutch Republic was independent, democratic, and largely Protestant, with no taste for saints and Madonnas.

Instead, Dutch burghers bought pretty, unpreachy, unpretentious works for their homes—still lifes (of food and mundane objects), landscapes, portraits (often of groups), and scenes from everyday life.

classical love garden, are other happy couples strolling arm-in-arm amid peacocks, a symbol of fertility.

In earlier times, marriage portraits put the man and wife in separate canvases, staring out grimly. Hals' jolly side-by-side couple reflects a societal shift from marriage as business partnership to an arrangement that's more friendly and intimate.

Hals didn't need symbolism to tell us that these two are prepared for their long-distance relationship—they seem relaxed together, but each looks at us directly, with a strong, individual identity. Good as gold, these

are the type of people who propelled this soggy little country into its glorious Golden Age.

▸ *A little farther along are the small-scale canvases of...*

Johannes Vermeer

Vermeer (1632-1675) is the master of tranquility and stillness. He creates a clear and silent pool that is a world in itself. Most of his canvases show interiors of Dutch homes, where Dutch women engage in everyday activities, lit by a side window.

Vermeer's father, an art dealer, gave Johannes a passion for painting. Late in the artist's career, with Holland drained by wars against England, the demand for art and luxuries went sour, forcing Vermeer to downsize—he sold his big home, packed up his wife and 14 children, and moved in with his mother-in-law. He died two years later, and his works fell into centuries of obscurity.

The Rijksmuseum has the best collection of Vermeers in the world—four of them. (There are only some 34 in captivity.) Each is a small jewel worth lingering over.

The Milkmaid, c. 1660

It's so quiet you can practically hear the milk pouring into the bowl.

Vermeer brings out the beauty in everyday things. The subject is ordinary—a kitchen maid—but you could look for hours at the tiny details and rich color tones. These are everyday objects, but they glow in a diffused light: the crunchy crust, the hanging basket, even the rusty nail in the wall with its tiny shadow. Vermeer had a unique ability with surface texture, to show how things feel when you touch them.

Vermeer's *Milkmaid*—quiet beauty

Woman Reading a Letter—from whom?

Shhh...Dutch Art

You're sitting at home late one night, and it's perfectly calm. Not a sound, very peaceful. And then...the refrigerator motor turns off, and it's really quiet.

Dutch art is really quiet art. It silences our busy world, so that every sound, every motion is noticeable. You can hear cows tearing off grass 50 yards away. You notice how the cold night air makes the stars sharp.

In fact, one of the museum's most dramatic, over-the-top paintings is probably *The Threatened Swan* (in the Gallery of Honor). It's quite a contrast to the rape scenes and visions of heaven of Italian Baroque paintings from the same time period.

The maid is alive with Vermeer's distinctive yellow and blue—the colors of many traditional Dutch homes—against a white backdrop. She is content, solid, and sturdy, performing this simple task as if it's the most important thing in the world. Her full arms are built with patches of reflected light. Vermeer squares off a little world in itself (framed by the table in the foreground, the wall in back, the window to the left, and the footstool at right), then fills this space with objects for our perusal.

***Woman Reading a Letter*, c. 1663**

Notice how Vermeer's placid scenes often have an air of mystery. The woman is reading a letter. From whom? A lover? A father on a two-year business trip to the East Indies? Not even taking time to sit down, she reads it intently, with parted lips and a bowed head. It must be important. (She looks pregnant, adding to the mystery, but that may just be the cut of her clothes.)

Again, Vermeer has framed a moment of everyday life. But within this small world are hints of a wider, wilder world—the light coming from the left is obviously from a large window, giving us a whiff of the life going on outside. The map hangs prominently, reminding us of travel, and perhaps of where the letter is from.

***The Love Letter*, c. 1669-1670**

There's a similar theme here. The curtain parts, and we see through the doorway into a dollhouse world, then through the seascape on the back

Vermeer's *The Love Letter*

Scene from the artist's hometown of Delft

wall to the wide ocean. A woman is playing a lute when she's interrupted by a servant bringing a letter. The mysterious letter stops the music, intruding like a pebble dropped into the pool of Vermeer's quiet world. The floor tiles create a strong 3-D perspective that sucks us straight into the center of the painting—the woman's heart.

***View of Houses in Delft,* a.k.a. *The Little Street,* c. 1658**

Vermeer was born in the picturesque town of Delft, grew up near its Market Square, and set a number of his paintings there. This may be the view from his front door.

The details in the painting actually aren't very detailed—the cobblestone street doesn't have a single individual stone in it. But Vermeer shows us the beautiful interplay of colored rectangles on the buildings. Our eye moves back and forth from shutter to gable to window...and then from front to back, as we notice the woman deep in the alleyway.

▸ *In an alcove nearby are some rollicking paintings by...*

Jan Steen

Not everyone could afford a masterpiece, but even poorer people wanted works of art for their homes (like a landscape from Sears for over the sofa). Jan Steen (c. 1625-1679, pronounced "yahn stain"), the Norman Rockwell of his day, painted humorous scenes from the lives of the lower classes. As a tavern owner, he observed society firsthand.

***The Feast of St. Nicholas,* 1665-1668**

It's Christmas time, and the kids have been given their gifts, including a little girl who got a doll. The mother says, "Let me see it," but the girl

Ruffs

I cannot tell you why men and women of the Dutch Golden Age found these fanlike collars attractive, but they certainly were all the rage here and elsewhere in Europe. It started in Spain in the 1540s, but the style really took off with a marvelous discovery in 1565: starch. Within decades, Europe's wealthy merchant class was wearing nine-inch collars made from 18 yards of material.

The ruffs were detachable and made from a long, pleated strip of linen set into a neck (or wrist) band. You tied it in front with strings. Big ones required that you wear a wire frame underneath for support. There were various types—the "cartwheel" was the biggest, a "double ruff" had two layers of pleats, and a "cabbage" was somewhat asymmetrical.

Ruffs required elaborate maintenance. First, you washed and starched the linen. While the cloth was still wet, hot metal pokers were painstakingly inserted into the folds to form the characteristic figure-eight pattern. The ruffs were stored in special round boxes to hold their shape.

For about a century, Europeans loved the ruff, but by 1630, Holland had come to its senses, and the fad faded.

turns away playfully. Everyone is happy except the boy, who's crying. His Christmas present is only a branch in his shoe—like coal in your stocking, the gift for bad boys. His sister gloats and passes it around. The kids laugh at him. But wait—it turns out the family is just playing a trick. In the background, the grandmother beckons to him, saying, "Look, I have your real present in here." Out of the limelight, but smack in the middle, sits the father providing ballast to this family scene and clearly enjoying his children's pleasure.

Steen has frozen the moment, sliced off a piece, and laid it on a

Steen—a rich burgher's moral dilemma

Steen—playful family scene at Christmas

canvas. He's told a story with a past, a present, and a future. These are real people in a real scene.

Steen's fun art reminds us that museums aren't mausoleums.

***The Merry Family,* 1668**

This family—three generations living happily under one roof—is eating, drinking, and singing like there's no tomorrow. The broken eggshells and scattered cookware symbolize waste and extravagance. The neglected proverb tacked to the fireplace reminds us that children will follow in the footsteps of their parents. The father in this jolly scene is very drunk—ready to topple over—while in the foreground his mischievous daughter is feeding her brother wine straight from the flask. Mom and Grandma join the artist himself (playing the bagpipes) in a lively sing-along, but the child learning to smoke would rather follow Dad's lead.

Dutch Golden Age families were notoriously lenient with their kids. Even today, the Dutch describe a rowdy family as a "Jan Steen household."

***Adolf and Catharina Croeser,* a.k.a. *The Burgomaster of Delft and His Daughter,* 1655**

Steen's well-dressed burgher sits on his front porch, when a poor woman and child approach to beg, putting him squarely between the horns of a moral dilemma. On the one hand, we see his rich home, well-dressed daughter, and a vase of flowers—a symbol that his money came from morally suspect capitalism (the kind that produced the folly of 1637's "tulip mania," described on page 31). On the other hand, there are his poor fellow citizens and the church steeple, reminding him of his Christian duty. The man's daughter avoids the confrontation. Will the burgher set the right

Steen's *Merry Family* may not be morally upright, but they sure know how to have fun.

Christian example? This moral dilemma perplexed many nouveau-riche Dutch Calvinists of Steen's day.

This early painting by Steen demonstrates his mastery of several popular genres: portrait, still life (the flowers and fabrics), cityscape, and moral instruction.

Rembrandt van Rijn

Rembrandt van Rijn (1606-1669) is the greatest of all Dutch painters. Whereas most painters specialized in one field—portraits, landscapes, still lifes—Rembrandt excelled in them all.

The son of a Leiden miller who owned a waterwheel on the Rhine ("van Rijn"), Rembrandt took Amsterdam by storm with his famous painting *The Anatomy Lesson of Dr. Nicolaes Tulp* (1632, currently in The Hague). The commissions poured in for official portraits, and he was soon wealthy and married (1634) to Saskia van Uylenburgh. They moved to an expensive home in the Jewish Quarter (today's Rembrandt's House museum—see page 128), and decorated it with their collection of art and exotic furniture.

His portraits were dutifully detailed, but other paintings explored strong contrasts of light and dark, with dramatic composition.

In 1642, Saskia died, and Rembrandt's fortunes changed, as the public's taste shifted and commissions dried up. In 1649, he hired an 18-year-old model named Hendrickje Stoffels, and she soon moved in with him and gave birth to their daughter.

Holland's war with England (1652-1654) devastated the art market, and Rembrandt's free-spending ways forced him to declare bankruptcy (1656)—the ultimate humiliation in success-oriented Amsterdam. The commissions came more slowly. The money ran out. His mother died. He had to auction off his paintings and furniture to pay debts. He moved out of his fine house to a cheaper place on Rozengracht. His bitter losses added a new wisdom to his work.

In his last years, his greatest works were his self-portraits, showing a tired, wrinkled man stoically enduring life's misfortunes. Rembrandt piled on layers of paint and glaze to capture increasingly subtle effects. In 1668, his lone surviving son, Titus, died, and Rembrandt passed away the next year. His death effectively marked the end of the Dutch Golden Age.

***Isaac and Rebecca,* a.k.a. *The Jewish Bride,* 1665-1669**

The man gently draws the woman toward him. She's comfortable enough with him to sink into thought, and she reaches up unconsciously to return the gentle touch. They're young but wizened. This uncommissioned portrait (its subjects remain unknown) is a truly human look at the relationship between two people in love. They form a protective pyramid of love amid a gloomy background. The touching hands form the center of this somewhat sad but peaceful work. Van Gogh said that "Rembrandt alone has that tenderness—the heartbroken tenderness."

Rembrandt was a master of oil painting. In his later years, he rendered details with a messier, more Impressionistic style. The red-brown-gold of the couple's clothes is a patchwork of oil laid on thick with a palette knife.

***The Wardens of the Amsterdam Drapers Guild,* a.k.a. *The Syndics,* 1662**

Rembrandt could paint an official group portrait better than anyone. In the painting made famous by Dutch Masters cigars, he catches the Drapers Guild in a natural but dignified pose (dignified, at least, until the guy on the left sits on his friend's lap).

It's a business meeting, and they're all dressed in black with black

Rembrandt's tender *Jewish Bride*

The Night Watch—Civic Guards in action

hats—the standard power suit of the Dutch Golden Age. They gather around a table examining the company's books. Suddenly, someone (us) walks in, and they look up. It's as natural as a snapshot, though X-rays show Rembrandt made many changes in posing them perfectly.

The figures are "framed" by the table beneath them and the top of the wood paneling above their heads, making a three-part composition that brings this band of colleagues together. Even in this simple portrait, we feel we can read the guild members' personalities in their faces. (If the table in the painting looks like it's sloping a bit unnaturally, lie on the floor to view it at Rembrandt's intended angle.)

▸ *At the far end of the Gallery of Honor stands the museum's star masterpiece. The best viewing spot is to the right of center—the angle Rembrandt had in mind when he designed it.*

The Night Watch, a.k.a. *The Militia Company of Captain Frans Banning Cocq,* 1642

This is Rembrandt's most famous—though not necessarily greatest—painting. Created in 1642, when he was 36, it was one of his most important commissions: a group portrait of a company of Amsterdam's Civic Guards to hang in their meeting hall.

It's an action shot. With flags waving and drums beating, the guardsmen (who, by the 1640s, were really only an honorary militia of rich bigwigs) spill onto the street from under an arch in the back. It's "all for one and one for all" as they rush to Amsterdam's rescue. The soldiers grab lances and load their muskets. In the center, the commander (in black, with a red sash) strides forward energetically with a hand gesture that seems to say, "What are we waiting for? Let's move out!" His lieutenant focuses on his every order.

Rembrandt caught the optimistic spirit of Holland in the 1600s. Its war of independence from Spain was heading to victory and the economy was booming. These guardsmen on the move epitomize the proud, independent, upwardly mobile Dutch.

Why is *The Night Watch* so famous? Compare it with other, less famous group portraits nearby, where every face is visible and everyone is well-lit, flat, and flashbulb-perfect. These people paid good money to have their mugs preserved for posterity, and they wanted it right up front. Other group portraits may be colorful, dignified works by a master...but not quite masterpieces.

By contrast, Rembrandt rousted the Civic Guards off their fat duffs. By adding movement and depth to an otherwise static scene, he took posers and turned them into warriors. He turned a simple portrait into great art.

OK, some *Night Watch* scuttlebutt: First off, "night watch" is a misnomer. It's a daytime scene, but over the years, as the preserving varnish darkened and layers of dirt built up, the sun set on this painting, and it got its popular title. When the painting was moved to a smaller room, the sides were lopped off (and the pieces lost), putting the two main characters in the center and causing the work to become more static than intended. During World War II, the painting was rolled up and hidden for five years. In 1975, a madman attacked the painting, slicing the captain's legs, and in 1990, it was sprayed with acid (it was skillfully restored after both incidents).

The Night Watch, contrary to popular myth, was a smashing success in its day. However, there are elements in it that show why Rembrandt soon fell out of favor as a portrait painter. He seemed to spend as much time painting the dwarf and the mysterious glowing girl with a chicken (the very appropriate mascot of this "militia" of shopkeepers) as he did the faces of his employers.

Rembrandt's life darkened long before his *Night Watch* did. This work marks the peak of Rembrandt's popularity...and the beginning of his fall from grace. He continued to paint masterpieces. Free from the dictates of employers whose taste was in their mouths, he painted what he wanted, how he wanted it. Rembrandt goes beyond mere craftsmanship to probe into, and draw life from, the deepest wells of the human soul.

▸ *Backtrack a few steps to the Gallery of Honor's last alcove to find Rembrandt's...*

***Self-Portrait as the Apostle Paul,* 1661**

Rembrandt's many self-portraits show us the evolution of a great painter's style, as well as the progress of a genius's life. For Rembrandt, the two were intertwined.

In this somber, late self-portrait, the man is 55 but he looks 70. With a lined forehead, a bulbous nose, and messy hair, he peers out from under several coats of glazing, holding old, wrinkled pages. His look is...skeptical? Weary? Resigned to life's misfortunes? Or amused? (He's looking at us, but not *just* at us—remember that a self-portrait is done staring into a mirror.)

This man has seen it all—success, love, money, fatherhood, loss, poverty, death. He took these experiences and wove them into his art. Rembrandt died poor and misunderstood, but he remained very much his own man to the end.

▸ *You'll find more Rembrandts in Room 2.8, located a half-dozen rooms to the left of* The Night Watch.

***Self-Portrait,* c. 1628**

Here we see the young small-town boy about to launch himself into whatever life has to offer. Rembrandt was a precocious kid. His father, a miller, insisted that he become a lawyer. His mother hoped he'd be a preacher (look for a portrait of her reading the Bible). Rembrandt combined the secular and religious worlds by becoming an artist, someone who can hint at the spiritual by showing us the beauty of the created world.

He moved to Amsterdam and entered the highly competitive art world. Amsterdam was a booming town and, like today, a hip and cosmopolitan city. Rembrandt portrays himself at age 22 as being divided—half

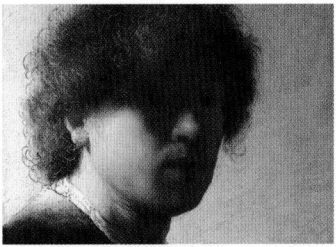

Young Rembrandt—what does his future hold?

Jeremiah—brooding in the darkness

in light, half hidden by hair and shadows—open-eyed, but wary of an uncertain future. Rembrandt's paintings are often light and dark, both in color and in subject, exploring the "darker" side of human experience.

***Portrait of a Woman, Possibly Maria Trip,* 1639**

This debutante daughter of a wealthy citizen is shy and reserved—maybe a bit awkward in her new dress and adult role, but still self-assured. When he chose to, Rembrandt could dash off a commissioned portrait like nobody's business. The details are immaculate—the lace and shiny satin, the pearls behind the veil, the subtle face and hands. Rembrandt gives us not just a person, but a personality.

Look at the red rings around her eyes, a detail a lesser painter would have airbrushed out. Rembrandt takes this feature, unique to her, and uses it as a setting for her luminous, jewel-like eyes. Without being prettified, she's beautiful.

***Young Woman in Fantasy Costume,* 1633**

As Rembrandt became known in Amsterdam, everyone wanted a portrait done by the young master, and he became wealthy and famous. He fell in love with and married the rich, beautiful, and cultured Saskia. By all accounts, the two were enormously happy, entertaining friends, decorating their house with fine furniture, raising a family, and living the high life. In this wedding portrait, thought to be of Saskia, the bride's face literally glows, and a dash of white paint puts a sparkle in her eye. Barely 30 years old, Rembrandt was the most successful painter in Holland. He had it all.

Maria Trip radiates honest beauty.

Self-portrait: These eyes have seen it all.

Bartholomeus Van der Helst's glorious group portrait is just one of many Golden Age treasures.

***Jeremiah Lamenting the Destruction of Jerusalem,* 1630**

The Babylonians have sacked and burned Jerusalem, but Rembrandt leaves the pyrotechnics (in the murky background at left) to Spielberg and the big screen. Instead, he tells the story of Israel's destruction in the face of the prophet who predicted the disaster. Jeremiah slumps in defeat, deep in thought, confused and despondent, trying to understand why this evil had to happen. Rembrandt turns his floodlight of truth on the prophet's deeply lined forehead.

Rembrandt wasn't satisfied to crank out portraits of fat merchants in frilly bibs, no matter what they paid him. He wanted to experiment, trying new techniques and more probing subjects. Many of his paintings weren't commissioned and were never even intended for sale. His subjects could be brooding and melancholy, a bit dark for the public's taste. His technique set him apart—you can recognize a Rembrandt canvas by his play of light and dark. Most of his paintings are a deep brown tone, with only a few bright spots glowing from the darkness. This allowed Rembrandt to highlight the details he thought most important and to express moody emotions.

More Golden Age Treasures

Welcome to the Dutch Golden Age. As you browse the rest of the second floor, look for...

Group Portraits: These men helped make Amsterdam the richest city on earth in the 1600s. Though shown in military uniforms, these men were really captains of industry—shipbuilders, seamen, salesmen, spice

Still life—the beauty of everyday things

The Rijks remembers the rich Golden Age.

tasters, bankers, and venture capitalists—all part of the complex economic web that planned and financed overseas trade.

Still Lifes: Savor the fruits of Holland's rich overseas trade—lemons from the south, pewterware from Germany, and spices from Asia. Pick a still life, and get so close that the guard joins you. You'll swear you can see yourself reflected in the pewter vessels. Linger over the little things—the closer you get the better they look. These carefully composed, photorealistic still-lifes capture the pride the Dutch had for their homes, which they cultivated like gardens to be immaculate, decorative, and in perfect order.

Artifacts: You'll see everyday items such as dollshouses *(poppenhuizen),* a ship's cannon, or a big wooden model of a 74-gun Dutch man-of-war that would have escorted convoys of merchant ships loaded with wealth.

The Rest of the Rijks

Most visitors are here to see the Golden Age art, but the museum has much, much more, with upward of 8,000 works on display—including a Van Gogh self-portrait (on the first floor), an airplane (third floor), women's fashion and delftware (lower level), and art from the East Indies, a former Dutch colony (Asian Art Pavilion).

Linger over these objects, appreciating the beauty of everyday things.

Van Gogh Museum Tour

The Van Gogh Museum (we say "van GO," the Dutch say "van hock") is a cultural high even for those not into art. Located near the Rijksmuseum, the museum houses the 200 paintings owned by Vincent's younger brother, Theo. It's a user-friendly stroll through the work and life of one enigmatic man. If you like brightly colored landscapes in the Impressionist style, you'll like this museum. If you enjoy finding deeper meaning in works of art, you'll really love it. The mix of Van Gogh's creative genius, his tumultuous life, and the traveler's determination to connect to it makes this museum as much a walk with Vincent as with his art.

ORIENTATION

Cost: €17.

Hours: Daily 9:00-18:00 (mid-July-Aug until 19:00), Fri until 22:00, Sat until 21:00 in mid-July-Aug–confirm evening hours before you visit.

Avoiding Lines: To get in without a wait, buy timed-entry tickets online at www.vangoghmuseum.com. If you have a Museumkaart or I Amsterdam card, you'll queue up at a shorter line than same-day ticket buyers.

When to Go: Midmornings are most crowded. Consider visiting on a Friday evening (or Saturday nights in summer), when crowds are sparse. On some Fridays, there are musicians or a DJ and a wine bar in the lobby.

Getting There: It's a few blocks behind the Rijksmuseum; visitors enter via a glass pavilion on the Museumplein. From Centraal station, catch tram #2 or #5 to the Rijksmuseum or Van Baerlestraat stop.

Getting In: There are separate lines for timed-entry ticket holders; those with a Museumkaart or I Amsterdam card; and new ticket buyers.

Information: Tel. 020/570-5200, www.vangoghmuseum.com.

Tours: The €5 multimedia guide gives insightful commentaries about Van Gogh's paintings, along with related quotations from Vincent himself.

Length of This Tour: Allow one hour.

Baggage Check: Free and mandatory.

Photography: No photos allowed.

Cuisine Art: The museum has a cafeteria-style café.

The Van Gogh Museum on Museumplein

Avoid crowds by visiting on Friday evening.

THE TOUR BEGINS

The collection is laid out roughly chronologically, divided into five periods of Vincent's life. Level 0—often displaying self-portraits—introduces you to the artist. Level 1 has his early paintings, level 2 focuses on the man and his contemporaries, and level 3 has his final works.

▸ *Pass through security and the ticket booth into the glass-pavilion reception hall, where you'll find an info desk, bag check, multimedia-guide rental, and WCs. Make your way up an escalator to the permanent collection, arriving on level 0.*

Vincent van Gogh, 1853-1890

I am a man of passions...

You could see Vincent van Gogh's canvases as a series of suicide notes—or

Self-portraits chronicle the stages of Vincent's life—his youth in Holland, Paris, Provence.

as the record of a life full of beauty...perhaps too full of beauty. He attacked life with a passion, experiencing highs and lows more intensely than the average person. The beauty of the world overwhelmed him; its ugliness struck him as only another dimension of beauty. He tried to absorb the full spectrum of experience, good and bad, and channel it onto a canvas. The frustration of this overwhelming task drove him to madness. If all this is a bit overstated—and I guess it is—it's an attempt to show the emotional impact that Van Gogh's works have had on many people, me included.

Vincent, a pastor's son from a small Dutch town, started working at age 16 as a clerk for an art dealership. But his two interests, art and religion, distracted him from his dreary work, and after several years, he was fired.

The next 10 years were a collage of dead ends as he traveled northern Europe pursuing one path after another. He launched into each project with incredible energy, then became disillusioned and moved on to something else: teacher at a boarding school, assistant preacher, bookstore apprentice, preacher again, theology student, English student, literature student, art student. He bounced around England, France, Belgium, and the Netherlands. He fell in love, but was rejected for someone more respectable. He quarreled with his family and was estranged. He lived with a prostitute and her daughter, offending the few friends he had. Finally, in his late twenties, worn out, flat broke, and in poor health, he returned to his family in Nuenen and made peace. He then started to paint.

▸ *Ascend to level 1. Work clockwise around the floor and follow the stages of Vincent's life. Start with his stark, dark early work.*

The Netherlands, 1880-1885

Poverty and Religion

These dark, gray canvases show us the hard, plain existence of the people and town of Nuenen, in the rural southern Netherlands. We see simple buildings, bare or autumnal trees, and overcast skies—a world where it seems spring will never arrive. What warmth there is comes from the sturdy, gentle people themselves.

The style is crude—Van Gogh couldn't draw very well and would never become a great technician. The paint is laid on thick, as though painted

with Nuenen mud. The main subject is almost always dead center, with little or no background, so there's a claustrophobic feeling. We are unable to see anything but the immediate surroundings.

***The Potato Eaters,* 1885**

Those that prefer to see the peasants in their Sunday-best may do as they like. I personally am convinced I get better results by painting them in their roughness...If a peasant picture smells of bacon, smoke, potato steam—all right, that's healthy.

In a dark, cramped room lit only by a dim lamp, poor workers help themselves to a steaming plate of potatoes. They've earned it. Vincent deliberately wanted the canvas to be potato-colored.

Vincent had dabbled as an artist during his wandering years, sketching things around him and taking a few art classes, but it wasn't until age 29 that he painted his first oil canvas. He soon threw himself into it with abandon.

He painted the poor working peasants. He worked as a lay minister among peasants and miners. He joined them at work in the mines, taught their children, and even gave away his own few possessions to help them. The church authorities finally dismissed him for "excessive zeal," but he came away understanding the poor's harsh existence and the dignity with which they bore it.

***Still Life with Bible,* 1885**

I have a terrible need of—shall I say the word?—religion. Then I go out and paint the stars.

The Bible and Émile Zola's *La Joie de Vivre*—these two books dominated Van Gogh's life. In his art he tried to fuse his religious upbringing with

Potato Eaters—the peasants he worked with

Still Life with Bible—son of a minister

his love of the world's beauty. He lusted after life with a religious fervor. The burned-out candle tells us of the recent death of his father. The Bible is open to Isaiah 53: "He was despised and rejected of men, a man of sorrows..."

***The Old Church Tower at Nuenen,* a.k.a. *The Peasants' Churchyard,* 1885**
The crows circle above the local cemetery of Nuenen. Soon after his father's death, Vincent—in poor health and depressed—moved briefly to Antwerp. He then decided to visit his brother Theo, an art dealer living in Paris, the art capital of the world. Theo's support—financial and emotional—allowed Vincent to spend the rest of his short life painting.

Vincent moved from rural, religious, poor Holland to Paris, the City of Light. Vincent van Gone.

▸ *Continue to the room with work he did in...*

Paris, March 1886-February 1888

Impressionism

The sun begins to break through, lighting up everything he paints. His canvases are more colorful and the landscapes more spacious, with plenty of open sky, giving a feeling of exhilaration after the closed, dark world of Nuenen.

In the cafés and bars of Paris' bohemian Montmartre district, Vincent met the revolutionary Impressionists. He roomed with Theo and became friends with other struggling young painters, such as Paul Gauguin and Henri de Toulouse-Lautrec. His health improved. He became more sociable, had an affair with an older woman, and was generally happy.

He signed up to study under a well-known classical teacher but quit after only a few classes. He couldn't afford to hire models, so he roamed the streets, sketch pad in hand, and learned from his Impressionist friends.

The Impressionists emphasized getting out of the stuffy studio and setting up canvases outside on the street or in the countryside to paint the play of sunlight off the trees, buildings, and water.

As you see in this room, at first, Vincent copied from the Impressionist masters. He painted garden scenes like Claude Monet, café snapshots like Edgar Degas, "block prints" like the Japanese masters, and self-portraits like...nobody else.

***Self-Portrait as a Painter*, 1887-1888**

I am now living with my brother Vincent, who is studying the art of painting with indefatigable zeal. –Theo van Gogh to a friend

Here, the budding young artist proudly displays his new palette full of bright new colors, trying his hand at the Impressionist technique of building a scene using dabs of different-colored paint. A whole new world of art—and life—opened up to him in Paris.

***Self-Portrait with Straw Hat*, 1887**

You wouldn't recognize Vincent, he has changed so much.... The doctor says that he is now perfectly fit again. He is making tremendous strides with his work.... He is also far livelier than he used to be and is popular with people.—Theo van Gogh to their mother

In Paris, Vincent learned the Impressionist painting technique. The shimmering effect comes from placing dabs of different colors side by side on the canvas. At a distance, the two colors blend in the eye of the viewer to become a single color. Here, Vincent uses separate strokes of blue, yellow, green, and red to create a brown beard—but a brown that throbs with excitement.

***Red Cabbages and Onions*, 1887**

Vincent quickly developed his own style: thicker paint; broad, swirling brushstrokes; and brighter, clashing colors that make even inanimate objects seem to pulsate with life. The many different colors are supposed to blend together, but you'd have to back up to Belgium to make these colors resolve into focus.

Church Tower, Nuenen—dark hometown scene

In Paris, the artist found bright colors.

***Self-Portrait with Gray Felt Hat*, 1887**

He has painted one or two portraits which have turned out well, but he insists on working for nothing. It is a pity that he shows no desire to earn some money because he could easily do so here. But you can't change people.—Theo van Gogh to their mother

Despite his new sociability, Vincent never quite fit in with his Impressionist friends. As he developed into a good painter, he became anxious to strike out on his own. He thought the social life of the big city was distracting him from serious work. In this painting, his face screams out from a swirling background of molecular activity. He wanted peace and quiet, a place where he could throw himself into his work completely. He headed for the sunny south of France.

▸ *Travel to the next room to reach...*

Arles, February 1888-May 1889

Sunlight, Beauty, and Madness

Winter was just turning to spring when Vincent arrived in Arles, near the French Riviera. After the dreary Paris winter, the colors of springtime overwhelmed him. The blossoming trees and colorful fields inspired him to paint canvas after canvas, drenched in sunlight.

***The Yellow House*, a.k.a. *The Street*, 1888**

It is my intention...to go temporarily to the South, where there is even more color, even more sun.

Vincent rented this house with the green shutters. (He ate at the pink café next door.) Look at that blue sky! He painted in a frenzy, working feverishly

With straw hat and pipe, he painted outdoors.

Traditional still life with modern colors

Thick brushstrokes radiate outward, magnifying the artist's ultra-intense gaze.

to try and take it all in. For the next nine months, he produced an explosion of canvases, working very quickly when the mood possessed him. His unique style evolved beyond Impressionism—thicker paint, stronger outlines, brighter colors (often applied right from the paint tube), and swirling brushwork that makes inanimate objects pulse and vibrate with life.

***The Bedroom,* 1888**

I am a man of passions, capable of and subject to doing more or less foolish things—which I happen to regret, more or less, afterwards.

Vincent was alone, a Dutchman in Provence. And that had its downside. He swung from flurries of ecstatic activity to bouts of great loneliness. Like anyone traveling alone, he experienced those high highs and low lows. This narrow, trapezoid-shaped, single-room apartment (less than 200 square feet) must have seemed like a prison cell at times. (Psychologists have pointed out that most everything in this painting comes in pairs—two chairs, two paintings, a double bed squeezed down to a single—indicating his desire for a mate. Hmm.)

He invited his friend Paul Gauguin to join him, envisioning a sort of artists' colony in Arles. He spent months preparing a room upstairs for Gauguin's arrival.

***Sunflowers,* 1889**

The worse I get along with people, the more I learn to have faith in Nature and concentrate on her.

Vincent saw sunflowers as his signature subject, and he painted a half-dozen versions of them, each a study in intense yellow. If he signed the work (look on the vase), it means he was proud of it.

Even a simple work like these sunflowers bursts with life. Different people see different things in *Sunflowers.* Is it a happy painting, or is it a melancholy one? Take your own emotional temperature and see.

***The Sower,* 1888**

A dark, silhouetted figure sows seeds in the burning sun. It's late in the day.

His *Yellow House* in sunny Arles

His bedroom, fit for the monastic artist

When Van Gogh signed a painting (like *Sunflowers*), it meant he was proud of it.

The heat from the sun, the source of all life, radiates out in thick swirls of paint. The sower must be a hopeful man, because the field looks slanted and barren. Someday, he thinks, the seeds he's planting will grow into something great, like the tree that slashes diagonally across the scene—tough and craggy, but with small, optimistic blossoms.

In his younger years, Vincent had worked in Belgium sowing the Christian gospel in a harsh environment (see Mark 4:1-9). Now in Arles, ignited by the sun, he cast his artistic seeds to the wind, hoping.

***Gauguin's Chair*, 1888**

Empty chairs—there are many of them, there will be even more, and sooner or later, there will be nothing but empty chairs.

Gauguin arrived. At first, they got along great, painting and carousing. But then things went sour. They clashed over art, life, and personalities. On Christmas Eve 1888, Vincent went ballistic. Enraged during an alcohol-fueled argument, he pulled out a razor and waved it in Gauguin's face. Gauguin took the hint and quickly left town. Vincent was horrified at himself. In a fit of remorse and madness, he mutilated his own ear and presented it to a prostitute.

The people of Arles realized they had a madman on their hands. A doctor diagnosed "acute mania with hallucinations," and the local vicar talked Vincent into admitting himself to a mental hospital. Vincent wrote to Theo: "Temporarily I wish to remain shut up, as much for my own peace of mind as for other people's."

▸ *Ascend to level 2, where you may see displays about Van Gogh's contemporaries as well as more Van Gogh paintings. The visit concludes on level 3, with Vincent's final paintings.*

St. Rémy, May 1889-May 1890

The Mental Hospital

In the mental hospital, Vincent continued to paint whenever he was well enough. He often couldn't go out, so he copied from books, making his own distinctive versions of works by Rembrandt, Delacroix, Millet, and others.

At first, the peace and quiet of the asylum did Vincent good, and his health improved. Occasionally, he was allowed outside to paint the gardens and landscapes. Meanwhile, the paintings he had been sending

Gauguin's Chair: When his friend visited, Vincent drove him away in a fit of madness.

to Theo began to attract attention in Paris for the first time. A woman in Brussels bought one of his canvases—the only painting he ever sold during his lifetime. In 1987, one of his *Sunflowers* sold for $40 million. Three years later a portrait of Vincent's doctor went for more than $80 million.

At St-Rémy, we see a change from bright, happy landscapes to more introspective subjects. The colors are less bright and more surreal, the brushwork even more furious. The strong outlines of figures are twisted and tortured.

***The Garden of Saint Paul's Hospital,* a.k.a. *Leaf Fall,* 1889**

...a traveler going to a destination that does not exist...

The stark brown trees are blown by the wind. A solitary figure (Vincent?) winds along a narrow, snaky path as the wind blows leaves on him. The colors are surreal—blue, green, and red tree trunks with heavy black outlines. A road runs away from us, heading nowhere.

***The Sheaf Binder, after Millet,* 1889**

I want to paint men and women with that something of the eternal which the halo used to symbolize...

Vincent's compassion for honest laborers remained constant. These sturdy folk, with their curving bodies, wrestle as one with their curving wheat. The world Vincent sees is charged from within by spiritual fires, twisting and turning matter into energy, and vice versa.

***Wheatfield with a Reaper,* 1889**

I have been working hard and fast in the last few days. This is how I try to express how desperately fast things pass in modern life.

Vincent portrays workers with noble dignity.

The fleeting glory of the *Almond Blossom*

The harvest is here. The time is short. There's much work to be done. A lone reaper works uphill, scything through a swirling wheat field, cutting slender paths of calm. Vincent saw the reaper—a figure of impending death—as the flip side of the sower.

***Pietà, after Delacroix,* 1889**

It's evening after a thunderstorm. Jesus has been crucified, and the corpse lies at the mouth of a tomb. Mary, whipped by the cold wind, holds her empty arms out in despair and confusion. She is the tender mother who receives us all in death, as though saying, "My child, you've been away so long—rest in my arms." Christ has a Vincent-esque red beard.

Auvers-sur-Oise, May-July 1890

The bird looks through the bars at the overcast sky where a thunderstorm is gathering, and inwardly he rebels against his fate. 'I am caged, I am caged, and you tell me I have everything I need! Oh! I beg you, give me liberty, that I may be a bird like other birds.' A certain idle man resembles this idle bird...

Though Van Gogh wished to be free of the mental hospital, his fits of madness would not relent. During these spells, he lost all sense of his own actions. He couldn't paint, the one thing he felt driven to do. He wrote to Theo, "My surroundings here begin to weigh on me more than I can say—I need air. I feel overwhelmed by boredom and grief."

***Almond Blossom,* 1890**

Vincent moved north to Auvers, a small town near Paris where he could stay under a doctor-friend's supervision. On the way there, he visited

This *Pietà* creates a mystical mood.

The trees ripple with an inner force.

Vincent's last painting, of a field like the one where he would end his short life

Theo. Theo's wife had just had a baby, whom they named Vincent. Brother Vincent showed up with this painting under his arm as a birthday gift. Theo's wife later recalled, "I had expected a sick man, but here was a sturdy, broad-shouldered man with a healthy color, a smile on his face, and a very resolute appearance." In his new surroundings, he continued painting, averaging a canvas a day, but was interrupted by spells that swung from boredom to madness. His letters to Theo were generally optimistic, but he worried that he'd soon succumb completely to insanity and never paint again. The final landscapes are walls of bright, thick paint.

***Wheatfield with Crows,* 1890**

This new attack...came on me in the fields, on a windy day, when I was busy painting.

On July 27, 1890, Vincent left his hotel, walked out to a nearby field, and put a bullet through his chest.

This is one of the last paintings Vincent finished. We can try to search the wreckage of his life for the black box explaining what happened, but there's not much there. His life was sad and tragic, but the record he left is one not of sadness, but of beauty—intense beauty. The windblown wheat field is a nest of restless energy. Scenes like this must have overwhelmed Vincent with their incredible beauty—too much, too fast, with no release. The sky is stormy and dark blue, almost nighttime, barely lit by two suns boiling through the deep ocean of blue. The road starts nowhere, leads nowhere, disappearing into the burning wheat field. Above all of this swirling beauty fly the crows, the dark ghosts that had hovered over his life since the cemetery in Nuenen.

Red Light District Walk

Amsterdam's oldest neighborhood has hosted the world's oldest profession since the Middle Ages. Today, prostitution and public marijuana use thrive here, creating a spectacle that's unique in all of Europe.

On our walk, we'll see history, sleaze, and cheese: transvestites in windows, drunks in doorways, and cannabis in bongs. The main event is sex: prostitutes in bras, thongs, and high heels, standing in window displays, offering their bodies—and it's all legal.

Not for Everyone: The Red Light District seems to have something to offend everyone. Whether it's in-your-face images of graphic sex, exploited immigrant women, whips and chains, passed-out drug addicts, the pungent smells of pot and urine, or just the shameless commercialism of it all, it's not everyone's cup of tea. And though I encourage people to expand their horizons, it's perfectly OK to say, "No, thank you."

ORIENTATION

Length of This Walk: Allow two hours.

Photography: Do not take photos of ladies in windows or a snarly bouncer may appear from out of nowhere to rip the camera from your hands. Photos of historic landmarks are OK, but remember that a camera or phone is a prime target in this high-theft area.

When to Go: Evenings (16:00-22:30) are lively with tourists, safe, and festive. Mornings are dead, and late night gets creepy.

Safety: The neighborhood is slowly gentrifying, and there are plenty of police, but also plenty of rowdy drunks, drug-pushing lowlifes, con artists, and pickpockets. Assume any fight or commotion is a ploy to distract innocent victims who are about to lose their wallets.

Old Church (Oude Kerk): €7.50 (credit cards only), Mon-Sat 10:00-18:00, Sun 13:00-17:30. Tower climb: €7.50 with 30-minute tour, April-Oct Mon-Sat 12:00-18:00.

Prostitution Information Center (PIC): €1, Wed-Fri 10:00-17:00 and Sat 10:00-19:00, closed Sun-Tue, €15 walking tours Sat at 17:00 and Wed at 18:30, tel. 020/420-7328, www.pic-amsterdam.com.

Amstelkring Museum: €10, Mon-Sat 10:00-17:00, Sun 13:00-17:00.

Cannabis College: Free, daily 11:00-19:00.

Hemp Gallery and Hash, Marijuana, and Hemp Museum: €9, daily 10:00-22:00.

Tours: 🎧 Download my free Red Light District audio tour.

THE WALK BEGINS

▸ *Start on Dam Square. Face the big, fancy Grand Hotel Krasnapolsky. To the left of the hotel stretches the long street called...*

❶ Warmoesstraat

You're walking along one of the city's oldest streets—the traditional border of the neighborhood tourists call the Red Light District.

Amsterdammers call this area De Wallen ("The Walls"), after the old retaining walls that once stood here. It's the oldest part of town, with the oldest church. It grew up between the harbor and Dam Square, where the city was born. A port town, Amsterdam traded in all kinds of goods,

Condom shop—be prepared.

Smartshops sell natural hallucinogens.

including things popular with sailors and businessmen away from home—like sex and drugs.

You'll pass the **Condomerie,** a condom store with flair. Located at the entrance to the Red Light District, this is the perfect place to get prepared.

Continue down Warmoesstraat. The two little street barricades with cute red lights around them mark the official entrance to the traffic-free world of De Wallen.

According to legend, Quentin Tarantino holed up at the **Winston Hotel** for three months in 1993 to write **Pulp Fiction.**

Notice all the **Irish pubs** and football matches on TVs in the bars. For Brits, Amsterdam is just a cheap flight away—perfect for a weekend getaway or stag party.

The small cross-street called **Wijde Kerksteeg** leads to the Old Church.

If you were to continue on Warmoesstraat, you'd come to **Elements of Nature** (at #97) "smartshop." This clean, well-lit, fully professional retail outlet sells powerful drugs, many of which are illegal in America. Because the drugs are "natural," the Dutch consider them beyond the reach of the law.

Smartshops sell everything from harmless nutrition boosters (such as royal jelly), to tobacco, herbal versions of popular dance-club drugs like Ecstasy, marijuana seeds, and hallucinogenic truffles. Prices are clearly marked, with descriptions of the drugs and their effects. The knowledgeable salespeople can give you more information on their "100 percent natural products that play with the human senses."

Farther down Warmoesstraat, you'd find a number of **sex shops** selling various erotic paraphernalia—dildos, S&M starter kits, and kinky magazines and videos. While Amsterdam is notorious for its Red Light District,

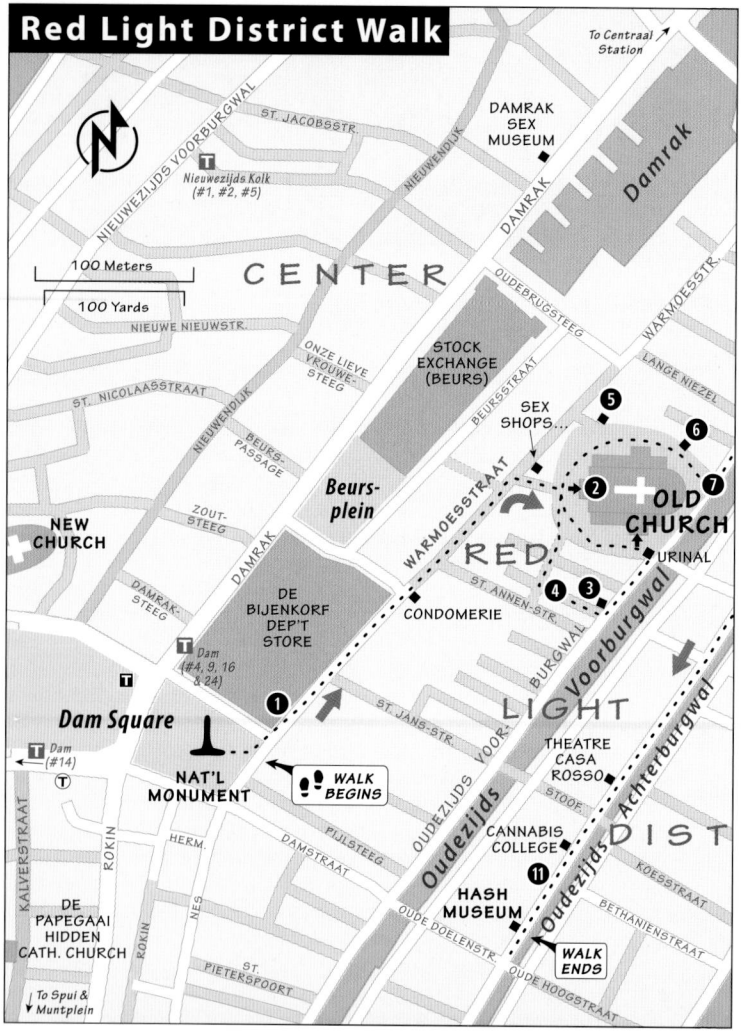
Red Light District Walk
To Centraal Station
DAMRAK SEX MUSEUM
Damrak
ST. JACOBSSTR.
NIEUWEZIJDS VOORBURGWAL
NIEUWENDIJK
Nieuwezijds Kolk (#1, #2, #5)
DAMRAK
100 Meters
100 Yards
CENTER
OUDEBRUGSTEEG
WARMOESSTR.
NIEUWE NIEUWSTR.
ONZE LIEVE VROUWE-STEEG
STOCK EXCHANGE (BEURS)
LANGE NIEZEL
ST. NICOLAASSTRAAT
BEURSSTRAAT
SEX SHOPS...
BEURS-PASSAGE
Beurs-plein
WARMOESSTRAAT
OLD CHURCH
NEW CHURCH
ZOUT-STEEG
URINAL
RED
DAMRAK-STEEG
DE BIJENKORF DEP'T STORE
ST. ANNEN-STR.
CONDOMERIE
Dam (#4, 9, 16 & 24)
Voorburgwal
BURGWAL
Dam Square
ST. JANS-STR.
LIGHT
Dam (#14)
THEATRE CASA ROSSO
NAT'L MONUMENT
WALK BEGINS
OUDEZIJDS VOOR-
Achterburgwal
STOOF
CANNABIS COLLEGE
DIST
HERM.
PULSTEEG
DAMSTRAAT
Oudezijds
KOESSTRAAT
KALVERSTRAAT
ROKIN
HASH MUSEUM
BETHANIENSTRAAT
DE PAPEGAAI HIDDEN CATH. CHURCH
NES
OUDE DOELENSTR.
WALK ENDS
ST PIETERSPOORT
OUDE HOOGSTRAAT
To Spui & Muntplein

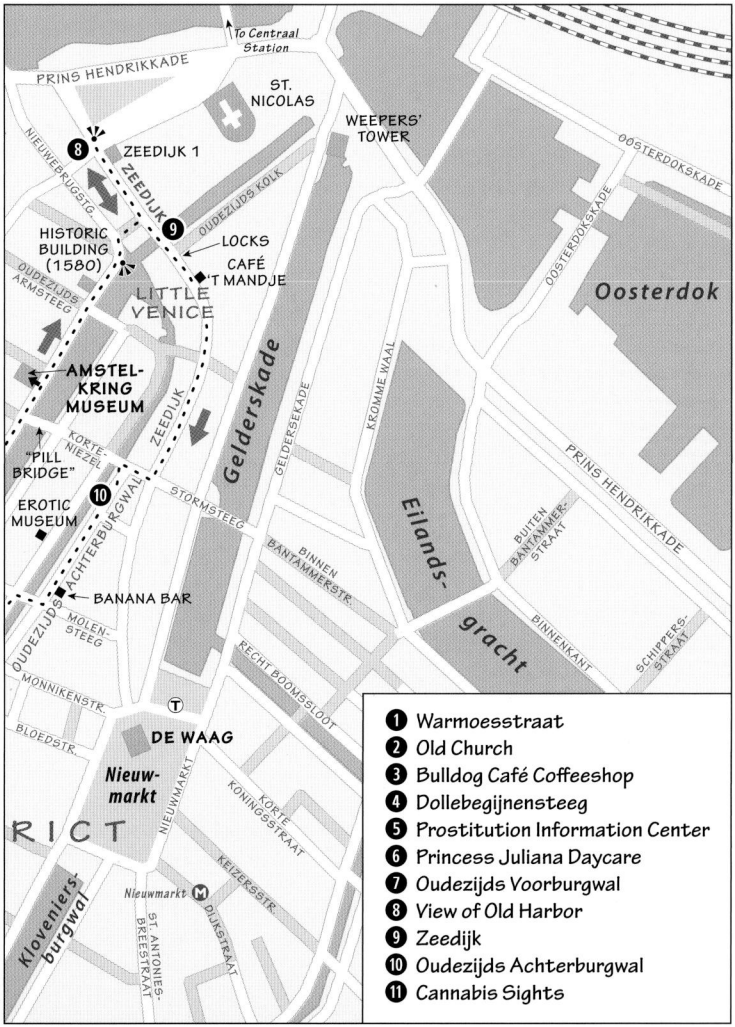
To Centraal Station
PRINS HENDRIKKADE
ST. NICOLAS
WEEPERS' TOWER
8
ZEEDIJK 1
NIEUWEBRUGSTR.
ZEEDIJK
9
OUDEZIJDS KOLK
OOSTERDOKSKADE
HISTORIC BUILDING (1580)
LOCKS
CAFÉ 't MANDJE
OUDEZIJDS ARMSTEEG
LITTLE VENICE
OOSTERDOKSKADE
Oosterdok
AMSTEL-KRING MUSEUM
Gelderskade
KROMME WAAL
GELDERSEKADE
ZEEDIJK
"PILL BRIDGE"
KORTE NIEZEL
PRINS HENDRIKKADE
10
EROTIC MUSEUM
ACHTERBURGWAL
STORMSTEEG
Eilands-gracht
BUITEN BANTAMMER-STRAAT
BINNEN BANTAMMERSTR.
BANANA BAR
MOLEN-STEEG
BINNENKANT
SCHIPPERS-STRAAT
OUDEZIJDS
MONNIKENSTR.
RECHT BOOMSSLOOT
T
BLOEDSTR.
DE WAAG
Nieuw-markt
NIEUWMARKT
KORTE KONINGSSTRAAT
RICT
KEIZERSSTR.
Nieuwmarkt
M
Kloveniers-burgwal
ST. ANTONIES-BREESTRAAT
DUKSTRAAT
1 Warmoesstraat
2 Old Church
3 Bulldog Café Coffeeshop
4 Dollebegijnensteeg
5 Prostitution Information Center
6 Princess Juliana Daycare
7 Oudezijds Voorburgwal
8 View of Old Harbor
9 Zeedijk
10 Oudezijds Achterburgwal
11 Cannabis Sights

even small Dutch towns often have a sex shop and a brothel to satisfy their citizens' needs.

▸ *But for now, let's go see the Old Church. Head down Wijde Kerksteeg to the...*

❷ Old Church (Oude Kerk)

As the name implies, this was the medieval city's original church. Returning from a long sea voyage, sailors of yore would spy the steeple of the Old Church on the horizon and know they were home. Having returned safely, they'd come here to give thanks to St. Nicholas—the patron saint of this church, of seafarers, of Christmas, and of the city of Amsterdam.

Church construction began in the early 1200s and continued in fits and starts for the next 200 years—as is apparent in the building's many gangly parts. Then, in the 15th century, Amsterdam built the New Church (Nieuwe Kerk) on Dam Square. But the Old Church still had the tallest spire and biggest organ, and it remained the city's center of activity, bustling inside and out with merchants and street markets.

The **tower** is 290 feet high, with an octagonal steeple atop a bell tower (you can pay to climb to the top). This tower served as the model for many other Dutch steeples. The carillon has 47 bells, which can chime mechanically or be played by one of Amsterdam's three official carillonneurs.

Circle to the right to the church entrance. While the church is historic, there's not much to see inside other than 2,500 gravestones in the floor (the most famous grave is for Rembrandt's wife, Saskia).

Nowadays, the church is the holy needle around which the unholy Red Light District spins. This marks the neighborhood's most dense concentration of prostitution.

Back outside, explore around the right side of the church. You'll see a **statue,** dedicated to the Unknown Prostitute. Attached to the church like barnacles are **small buildings.** These were originally used as homes for priests, church offices, or rental units. The house to the right of the entrance (at #25) is very tiny—32 feet by 8 feet. (An elderly lady lives in the house at #19 and doesn't like tourists, so be discreet.)

Now check out the green metal **urinal** over by the canal. This one gets a lot of use.

▸ *From the urinal, go a half-block south along the canal toward the...*

Old Church—historic charm amid the sleaze

Statue honoring the Unknown Prostitute

❸ Bulldog Café Coffeeshop

The Bulldog claims to be Amsterdam's very first marijuana coffeeshop, established here in 1975. Now there's a chain of Bulldogs around the city. At "coffeeshops" like this one, customers start the transaction by asking the bartender, "Can I see the cannabis menu?" Then the bartender pulls out a display case with different varieties of weed, sold in baggies or prerolled joints. It's all clearly priced, and available either to-go or to smoke on the premises. You'll see people at the Bulldog enjoying a joint while they sip a beer or a Coke.

As coffeeshops go, the Bulldog is considered pretty touristy, meant for young foreigners. Connoisseurs prefer smaller places with better-quality pot and a mellower ambience.

In recent years, various Dutch politicians have proposed new laws that would forbid sales of marijuana to nonresidents. But many Amsterdam businesses depend on out-of-town stoners for their livelihood. The current mayor of Amsterdam is adamant that the city's coffeeshops will remain open.

▸ *Time to dive into the heart of the Red Light District—the world of legal prostitution. Immediately adjacent to the coffeeshop is a three-foot-wide entrance to a narrow alleyway called...*

❹ Dollebegijnensteeg

You're right in the thick of high-density prostitution. Remember: Don't take any pictures, and watch for pickpockets if crowds jostle together. If you do both these things, you'll be fine.

As you pass window after window of women in panties and bras, notice how they wink at the horny men, rap on the window to attract

Marijuana coffeeshop—no big deal here

Narrow alley with prostitutes in windows

attention, or look disdainfully at sightseers. You can take your time here and then explore deeper (or you can hurry to the end of the block and turn right to return to the Old Church).

▸ *Return to the Old Church and start to circle the church clockwise. Around the back, you'll see older, plumper (and cheaper) prostitutes. In the same area, at Enge Kerksteeg 3, is the...*

❺ Prostitution Information Center (PIC) and Room-Rental Office

This PIC exists solely to demystify prostitution, giving visitors matter-of-fact information on how the trade works and what it's like to be a sex worker. It doles out pamphlets, books, condoms, T-shirts, and other offbeat souvenirs, and offers a twice-weekly walking tour.

Next door is a **room-rental office** (labeled *Kamerverhuurbedrijf*). Prostitutes come here to rent window space and bedrooms to use for their work. Several of the available rooms for rent are just next door. The office also sells supplies—condoms by the case, toilet tissue, lubricants, and soft drinks. The man at the desk does not arrange sex. The women who rent space from this business are self-employed and negotiate directly with their customers.

In return for their rental fees, prostitutes get security. The man in the office keeps an eye on them by video surveillance—you can see the monitors inside. Looking along the street, notice the small cameras and orange alarm lights above the doors. If prostitutes have any trouble, they press a buzzer that swiftly calls a burly bouncer or the police. The area sure looks rough, but, aside from tricky pickpockets, these streets are actually pretty safe.

▸ *Continue circling clockwise around the church. Amid prostitutes in*

Red Light areas have strict security video.

The "PIC" has info about the sex trade.

windows, find the white brick building on the left at Oudekerksplein 8. This is the...

❻ Princess Juliana Daycare

De Wallen is also a residential neighborhood, where ordinary citizens go about their daily lives. Of course, locals need someplace to send their kids. The Princess Juliana Daycare is for newborns to four-year-olds. It was built in the 1970s, when the idea was to mix all dimensions of society together, absorbing the seedy into the decent. I don't know about you, but this location would be a tough sell where I come from.

▸ *Turn left at the canal and continue north along...*

❼ Oudezijds Voorburgwal and Pill Bridge

Pause at Pill Bridge and enjoy the canal and all the old buildings with their charming gables. Back in the 1970s, this bridge was nicknamed for the retail items sold by the seedy guys who used to hang out here. Now it's a pleasant place for a photo op.

Just past the bridge, at Oudezijds Voorburgwal 38, is one of the city's most worthwhile sights: the **Amstelkring Museum** and Our Lord in the Attic Church. With its triangular gable, this building looks like just another townhouse. But inside, it holds a secret—a small, lavishly decorated place of worship hidden in the attic. Although Amsterdam has long been known for its tolerance, back in the 16th and 17th centuries there was one group they kept in the closet—Catholics. (For more, see page 118.)

As we stroll up the canal, remember that this neighborhood is Amsterdam's oldest. It sits on formerly marshy land that was reclaimed by diking off the sea's tidal surge. That location gave Amsterdam's merchants

Prostitution in Amsterdam

A customer browses around. A prostitute catches his eye. If the prostitute is interested in his business (prostitutes are selective for their own safety), she winks him over. They talk at the door as she explains her price and what she has to offer. Many are very aggressive at getting the man inside, where the temptation game revs up. A price is agreed on and paid in advance. A typical visit can cost €30-50 for a promised 20 minutes. The man goes in. The woman draws the curtain. Where do they actually do it? The rooms look tiny from the street, but these are just display windows. There's a bigger room behind or upstairs that comes with a bed, a sink, and not much else (or so I've heard). The average time for a visit: about 10 minutes.

Are there male prostitutes? Certainly—anything you might want is available somewhere in the Red Light District. But an experiment

easy access to both river trade and the North Sea. Brave Dutch sailors traveled to Africa, America, and Asia, returning with shiploads of exotic goods. The **historical building** (at #14) is from Amsterdam's glory years—around 1580.

With its canals and fine townhouses, Amsterdam became known as the "Venice of the North." The part of the canal we're walking along now is known as **"Little Venice."** Houses rise directly from the water here, with no quays or streets.

▸ *At the end of the canal, continue straight up a small inclined lane called Sint Olofssteeg. At the top, turn left and walk along a street called Zeedijk about 100 yards to the end of the block, where it opens up to an...*

❽ Old Harbor View and Old Wooden House

As you survey the urban scene of today's Damrak and Centraal station,

in the 1990s to put male prostitutes in windows didn't stand up. The district does, however, have plenty of transvestites, who advertise with blue lights rather than red.

The prostitutes here are self-employed—entrepreneurs, renting space and running their own business. They usually work a four- to eight-hour shift. A good spot costs about €100 for a day shift, and €150 for an evening. Prostitutes are required to keep their premises hygienic, make sure their clients use condoms, and avoid minors.

Popular prostitutes can make about €500 a day. They fill out tax returns, and many belong to a loose union called the Red Thread. The law, not pimps, protects prostitutes. If a prostitute is diagnosed with HIV or AIDS, she loses her license. As shocking as legalized prostitution may seem to some, it's a good example of a pragmatic Dutch solution to a persistent problem.

Although some women choose prostitution as a lucrative career, others (likely most) are forced into it by circumstance—poverty, drug addiction, abusive men, and immigration scams. While the hope is that sex workers are smartly regulated small-businesspeople, in reality the line between victim and entrepreneur is not always so clear.

imagine the scene as it looked in the 1600s. What today is mostly concrete was once the city's harbor. Boats sailed in and out of the harbor through an opening located where the train station sits now (on reclaimed land). From there, ships could sail along the IJ River out to the North Sea.

The **old wooden house**—now a café—was once a tavern, sitting right at what was then the water's edge.

It was a bustling port. Amsterdam became home to the Dutch East India Company, the world's first multinational corporation. Goods from all over the world flowed into this harbor, from where cargo was transferred to smaller river-trade boats that sailed up the Amstel to Europe's interior. The city grew wealthier and larger, expanding beyond De Wallen to new neighborhoods to the west and south. In its Golden Age, Amsterdam was perhaps the wealthiest city on earth, known as the "warehouse of the world."

Picture a ship tying up in the harbor. The crew has just returned

Pill Bridge, near quaint Little Venice

Pioneering gay bar along Zeedijk street

home from a two-year voyage to Bali. They're bringing home fabulous wealth—crates and crates of spices, coffee, and silk. Sailors celebrate their homecoming, spilling onto the Zeedijk. They're greeted by swinging ladies swinging red lanterns. They stop into St. Olaf's chapel to say a prayer of thanks—then head straight to this tavern at Zeedijk 1 and drop anchor for a good Dutch beer. Ahh-hh!

▸ *But our journey continues on. Backtrack along the same street, to the crest of a bridge, to take in the...*

❾ Zeedijk

This waterway is part of the city's system of **locks:** Once a day a worker opens up a box here and presses a button. The locks open, and the tides flush out the city's canals. Look down—if the gate is open, you might see water flowing in or out. The Zeedijk runs along the top of the "sea dike" that historically protected sea-level Amsterdam from the North Sea tides.

In the early 1600s, Zeedijk street was thriving with overseas trade. But as Amsterdam lost its maritime supremacy to England and France, De Wallen languished. By the 1970s the Zeedijk had become unbelievably sleazy. When I made my first trip here, this street was nicknamed "Heroin Alley." Thousands of addicts wandered like zombies and squatted in old buildings. It was a no-man's-land of junkies fighting among themselves, and the police just kept their distance.

But locals took back this historic corner of their city. The first step was legalizing marijuana, followed by a harsh crackdown on hard drugs—heroin, cocaine, and pills. Almost overnight, the illicit drug trade dropped dramatically. Dealers got stiff sentences. Addicts got treatment. Four decades

later, the policy seems to have worked, and the Zeedijk belongs to the people of Amsterdam once again.

▸ *Continue down the Zeedijk.*

The **Café 't Mandje** (at #63) was one of Europe's first gay bars, opened in 1927. Today it stands as a memorial to Bet van Beeren, who ran the bar during its heyday in the 1950s and '60s. Bet was a lesbian (the original Zee-dyke), and her bar became a safe hangout for gay people. Neckties hang from the ceiling, a reminder of Bet's tradition of scissoring off customers' ties.

▸ *Round the bend on Zeedijk street. Then turn right on narrow Korte Stormsteeg street. This leads quickly back to the canalside red lights. Then go left, walking along the left side of the canal.*

⑩ Oudezijds Achterburgwal

We're back in the glitzy Red Light District. This beautiful, tree-lined canal is the heart of this neighborhood's nightlife, playing host to most of the main nightclubs.

The **Banana Bar** (Bananenbar, at #78)—with its erotic Art Nouveau

Scenic canals and sex shows

Social Control

De Wallen has pioneered the Dutch concept of "social control." In Holland, neighborhood security doesn't come from just the police, but from neighbors looking out for each other. If Geert doesn't buy bread for two days, the baker asks around if anyone's seen him. An elderly man feels safe in his home, knowing he's being watched over by the prostitutes next door. Unlike many big cities, there's no chance that anyone here could die or be in trouble and go unnoticed. Video-surveillance cameras keep an eye on the streets. So do prostitutes, who buzz for help if they spot trouble. As you stroll, watch the men who watch the women who watch out for their neighbors—"social control."

facade—is, basically, a strip club with a-peel: For €60 you get admission for an hour, drinks included. Undressed ladies serve the drinks, perched on the bar. Touching is not allowed, but you can order a banana, and the lady will serve it to you, any way you like. For a full description, step into the lobby.

Pause and look to the right. The **Erotic Museum** (at #54) is a sex museum that's not as good as the Damrak Sex Museum (see page 120). However, it does use instructional mannequins to show some of the sex services found in the Red Light District (a prostitute's chambers, an S&M tableau).

At Molensteeg, cross the bridge and turn left. Continue south along Oudezijds Achterburgwal. **Theatre Casa Rosso** (lined by pink elephants) is a legit operation. Customers pay a single admission price (no rip-offs or hidden charges) for a strip show. The main event is naked people on stage engaging in sex acts—some simulated, some completely real (€40, www.casarosso.nl).

As you continue south along the canal, you gotta wonder: Why does Amsterdam embrace prostitution and drugs? It's not that the Dutch are any more liberal in their attitudes—they aren't. They're simply more pragmatic. They've found that when the sex trade goes underground, you get pimps, mobsters, and the spread of STDs. When marijuana is illegal, you get drug dealers, gangs, and violent turf wars. Their solution is to keep these markets legal, and minimize problems through strict regulation.

▸ *But enough about sex. Let's talk about drugs. (Don't worry, our walk*

is nearly over.) Along the right side of the next block, you'll find four cannabis-related establishments.

⓫ Cannabis Sights

Certain strains of the cannabis plant—particularly mature females of the species *sativa* and *indica*—contain the psychoactive alkaloid tetrahydrocannabinol (THC) that makes you high. The buds, flowers, and leaves (marijuana) can be dried and smoked. The brown sap/resin/pitch that oozes out of the leaves (hashish, a.k.a. hash) can also be dried and smoked. Both produce effects ranging from euphoria to paranoia to the munchies.

The **Cannabis College** (at #124) is a free, nonprofit public study center designed to explain the pros and cons (but mostly pros) of the industrial, medicinal, and recreational uses of the green stuff. You can read about practical hemp products, the medical uses of marijuana, and police prosecution/persecution of cannabis users. Most interesting, you can go downstairs (€3) to see a small cannabis garden.

In the evening, the area is safe and festive.

Several sights teach about marijuana...

...and its notorious history.

The **Hemp Gallery** (at #130, admission included in Museum ticket, next) extols the wonders of industrial hemp.

The **Hash, Marijuana, and Hemp Museum** (at #148) treats marijuana like it deserves scholarly study. The exhibits are quite extensive and interesting.

Throughout history, various peoples have used cannabis as a sacred ritual drug—from ancient Scythians and Hindus to modern Nepalis and Afghanis. Modern Rastafarians, following a Bible-based religion centered in Jamaica, smoke cannabis, bob to reggae music, and praise God. All over Amsterdam, you'll see the Rastafarian colors: green, gold, and red, mon.

The museum's highlight is the grow room, where you look through windows at live cannabis plants, some as tall as I am. At a certain stage they're "sexed" to weed out the boring males and "selected" to produce the most powerful strains.

At the museum's exit you'll pass through the **Sensi Seed Bank Store,** which sells weed seeds, how-to books, and knickknacks geared to growers.

Congratulations

We've seen a lot. We've peeked at locals—from prostitutes to drug pushers to the ghosts of pioneer lesbians to politically active heads with green thumbs. We've talked a bit of history, a little politics, and a lot of sleaze. Congratulations. You've survived. Now, go back to your hotel and take a shower.

Jordaan Walk

This walk takes you from Dam Square—the Times Square of Amsterdam—to the Anne Frank House, and then deep into the characteristic Jordaan neighborhood. Cafés, boutiques, bookstores, and art galleries have gentrified the area. On this cultural scavenger hunt, you'll experience the laid-back Dutch lifestyle and catch a few intimate details that most busy tourists never appreciate. You'll see things in the Jordaan (yor-DAHN) that are commonplace in no other city in the world.

Allow about 90 minutes for this short and easygoing walk. It's best by day (before 18:00), when views are nice, and shops and sights are open. (St. Andrew's Courtyard is closed on Sundays.) 🎧 You can download this chapter as a free Rick Steves audio tour. Bring your camera, as you'll enjoy some of Amsterdam's most charming canal scenes.

THE WALK BEGINS

❶ Dam Square

Start in Dam Square, where the city was born (for more on this square, see page 19). The original residents settled east of here, in the De Wallen neighborhood (now the Red Light District). But as Amsterdam grew—from a river-trading village to a worldwide sea-going empire—the population needed more housing. Citizens started reclaiming land to the west of Dam Square, creating new waterways lined with merchants' townhouses and building a "new church" (Nieuwe Kerk) to serve these new neighborhoods. (This is the area we'll be walking through in the first half of our tour.)

By the 1600s—Amsterdam's Golden Age—residents needed still more land. They opened up a new development farther west, the Jordaan. It was served by a new church to the west—the Westerkerk, which we'll see. It was also in the 1600s that the Royal Palace was built here on Dam Square. It didn't house royalty, as the name suggests, but was home to the city council. They passed zoning laws and oversaw the rapid expansion of this growing metropolis. Now, let's go see it.

▸ *Facing the Royal Palace, slip to the right, between the palace and the New Church. You'll soon see the facade of a red brick building. When it was built in 1899, Amsterdam's old post office was constructed atop a foundation of 4,500 pilings. This building, ultra modern in its day, remained Amsterdam's main post office until the 1980s; now it's the Magna Plaza mall.*

Facing Magna Plaza, head right, walking 50 yards down the busy street to the corner of a tiny street called...

❷ Molsteeg

Scan the higgledy-piggledy facades across the busy street. Are you drunk, high...or just in Amsterdam, where the houses were built on mud? Check out the nice line of gables along Molsteeg.

Notice the T-shirt gallery on the corner. Decades ago, I bought a Mark Raven T-shirt from a street vendor. Now this Amsterdam original, an artist with a distinctive spindly-lined style, has his own upscale shop.

▸ *Now head left down tiny Molsteeg street—but don't walk on the reddish pavement in the middle; that's for bikes. From here this tour's essentially a straight shot west, though the street changes names along the way.*

Start on Dam Square, face west, and walk.

Molsteeg is bike-friendly (so watch out!).

A few steps along, on the left, find house #5: It's from 1644. Just one window wide, it's typical of the city's narrow old merchants' houses, with a shop on the ground floor, living space in the middle, and storage in the attic. Look up to see the hooks above warehouse doors. Houses lean out on purpose, so you can hoist up cargo without banging it against the house.

At the intersection with Spuistraat, you'll likely see rows of **bicycles** parked along the street. Amsterdam's 820,000 residents own nearly that many bikes. Bikes outnumber cars here. Many people own two bikes—a long-distance racing bike and an in-city bike, often deliberately kept in poor maintenance so it's less enticing to the many bike thieves in town. Locals are diligent about locking their bikes twice: first the spokes, then a heavy chain attaching the bike to something immovable, such as a city hitching rack.

The efficient Dutch appreciate a self-propelled machine that travels five times faster than a person on foot, while creating zero pollution, noise, parking problems, or high fuel costs. On a *fiets* (bike), a speedy local can traverse the historic center in about 10 minutes. Biking seems to keep the populace fit and good-looking—people here say that Amsterdam's health clubs are more for networking than for working out.

▸ *The street opens onto a small space that's actually a bridge, straddling the Singel canal. It's called...*

❸ Torensluis Bridge

We haven't quite reached the Jordaan yet, but the atmosphere already seems miles away from busy Dam Square. With cafés, art galleries, and fine benches for picnics, this is a great place to have a seat and take in a Golden Age atmosphere.

Singel Canal: This canal was the original moat running around the old walled city, and this wide bridge was a road to the city gate.

The Houses: Many of these stately townhouses are from the 1600s, when Amsterdam was awash in overseas wealth, the city was expanding, and rich merchants were moving into this new, exclusive neighborhood.

The houses crowd together, shoulder-to-shoulder. They're built on top of thousands of logs hammered vertically into the marshy soil to provide a foundation. Over the years, they've shifted with the tides, leaving some leaning this way and that. Notice that some of the brick houses have iron rods strapped onto the sides. These act like braces, binding the bricks to an inner skeleton of wood. Almost all Amsterdam houses have big, tall windows to let in as much light as possible.

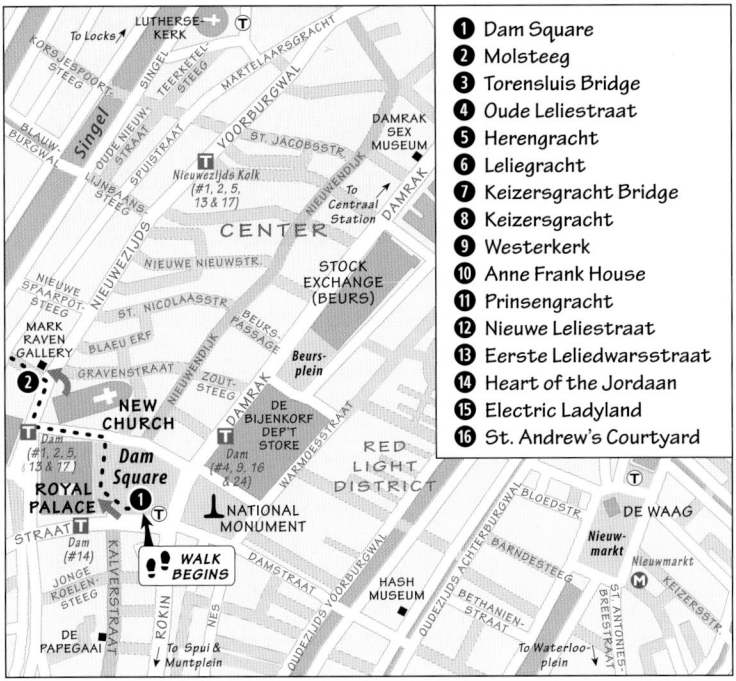

Although some houses look quite narrow, most of them extend far back, into an *achterhuis.* As owners were once taxed by the amount of street frontage, it made sense to build up and back.

Multatuli: The "big head" statue honors a writer known by his pen name, Multatuli. Born in Amsterdam in 1820, Multatuli (a.k.a. Eduard Douwes Dekker) did what many young Dutchmen did back then: He sought his fortune in the East Indies, then a colony of the Netherlands. He witnessed firsthand the hard life of Javanese natives slaving away on Dutch-owned plantations. His semi-autobiographical novel, *Max Havelaar* (1860), raised awareness of Dutch colonial abuses. For his talent and subject matter, Multatuli has been dubbed "the Dutch Rudyard Kipling."

The Locks: In the distance, way down at the north end of the Singel,

Playful Jordaan residents

Torensluis Bridge—cafés and views

beyond the copper dome (a Lutheran church), you can glimpse one of the canal's locks. Those white-flagpole thingies, sprouting at 45-degree angles, are part of the apparatus that opens and shuts the gates. While the canals originated as a way to drain diked-off marshland, they eventually became part of the city's sewer system. They were flushed daily: Just open the locks, and let the North Sea tides come in and out.

The Dutch are credited with inventing locks in the 1300s. (Let's not tell the ancient Chinese.) Besides controlling water flow in the city, they allow ships to pass from higher to lower water levels, and vice versa. It's because of locks that you can ship something by boat from here inland. From this very spot, you could hop a boat and go upriver, connect to the Rhine, then the Danube (over the continental divide in Germany), and then sail down the Danube, finally reaching the Black Sea and Romania.

▸ *Continue west on...*

❹ Oude Leliestraat

On "Old Lily Street," consumers will find plenty of Amsterdam treats—Reypenaer's cheeses, Puccini's bonbons, Tuscany's sausages, Grey Area's marijuana, California's burritos, sushi, and *shoarmas*—everything but lilies. The Reypenaer cheese shop is especially worthwhile, as it offers samples and tasting sessions (for a fee, reserve at 020/320-6333, www.wijngaardkaas.nl).

The Grey Area's green-and-white decal in the window identifies it as #092 in the city's licensing program for marijuana-dealing "coffeeshops." While smoking marijuana is essentially legal here, the café's name refers to the murky back side of the marijuana business—how coffeeshops get their supply from wholesalers. That's the "gray area" that Dutch laws have yet to

Gables

Along the rooftops, Amsterdam's famous gables are false fronts to enhance roofs that are, generally, sharply pitched. Gables come in all shapes and sizes. They might be ornamented with animal and human heads, garlands, urns, scrolls, and curlicues. Despite their infinite variety, most belong to a few distinct types. See how many of these you can spot.

A simple "point" gable just follows the triangular shape of a normal pitched roof. A "bell" gable is shaped like...well, guess. "Step" gables are triangular in shape and lined with steps. The one with a rectangular protrusion at the peak is called a "spout" gable. "Neck" gables rise up vertically from a pair of sloping "shoulders." "Cornice" gables make pointed roofs look classically horizontal. (There's probably even a "clark" gable, but frankly, I don't give a damn.)

See no reefer, hear no reefer at Grey Area.

Herengracht—a canal of gabled townhouses

sort out. This esteemed coffeeshop, which works with the best boutique growers in Holland, regularly wins big at Amsterdam's annual Cannabis Cup Awards—a "high" honor, to be sure.

▸ *The next canal is the...*

❺ Herengracht

Amsterdam added this canal during its Dutch Golden Age boom in the 1600s. It's named for the *heren,* the wealthy city merchants who lined it with their mansions. Even today, this is a high-rent district. (Zoning here forbids houseboats.)

Check out the house that's kitty-corner across the bridge, at Herengracht 150. It has features you'll find on many old Amsterdam buildings. On the roof, rods support the false-front gable. From this side view, you can see that, though a townhouse might have a narrow entrance, it can stretch far back from the street.

Find the parking sign along Herengracht (on the left) instructing motorists to put money in the meter at the end of the block. Parking is a major problem in a city like this, designed for boats, not cars.

▸ *Continue west, walking along...*

❻ Leliegracht

This is one of the city's prettiest small canals, lined with trees and lanterns, and crossed by a series of arched bridges. There are some 400 such bridges in Amsterdam. It's a pleasant street of eccentric boutiques, trendy furniture shops, and bookstores.

Notice that some buildings have staircases leading down below the street level to residences. Looking up, you'll see the characteristic beams

jutting out from the top with a cargo-hoisting hook on the end. The view from a bay window here must be exceptional.

▸ *Continue on to the next canal and pause on the* ❼ ***Keizersgracht Bridge*** *to take in the view. There's a fine row of gables, and the colorful crown of the Westerkerk church tower rises above the rooftops.*

After the bridge, we'll take a detour off our westward route, and veer left along...

❽ Keizersgracht

Walk south about 100 yards along the canal.

Homomonument: You'll reach a set of steps leading down to the water, where a triangular pink stone juts into the canal. This is part of the so-called Homomonument, Amsterdam's memorial to homosexuals who lost their lives in World War II, and a commemoration of all those persecuted for their sexuality. If you survey the square, you'll see that the pink triangle is just one corner of a larger triangle that comprises the entire Homomonument. These are contained in a single large triangle that comprises the Homomonument. (The pink-triangle design reclaims the symbol that the Nazis used to mark homosexuals.) You may see flowers or cards left here by friends and loved ones.

Westermarkt Square: In the square between the church and busy Raadhuisstraat, you'll find three very Dutch kiosks. The first, called Pink Point, gives out information on gay and lesbian Amsterdam. The next sells French fries; when it's closed, the shutters feature funny paintings putting *friets* into great masterpieces of Western art. The final one sells fresh herring. Try one. You get a fresh herring with pickles and onion on a paper plate and instructions from the friendly merchant on how to eat it.

The cute little **statue** is of Anne Frank, who holed up with her family in a house just down the block from here.

▸ *For now, turn your attention to the impressive...*

❾ Westerkerk

Look up at the towering spire. The crown shape was a gift of the Habsburg emperor, Maximilian I. As a thanks for a big loan, the city got permission to use the Habsburg royal symbol. The tower also displays the symbol of Amsterdam, with its three Xs.

The Westerkerk (Western Church) was built in 1631, as the city was expanding out from Dam Square. Rembrandt's buried inside...but no one

A memorial to AIDS victims

The crown of the Westerkerk

knows where. You can pop into the church for free, or pay to climb to the tower balcony (just below the *XXX*) for a grand view (church generally open April-Sept Mon-Fri 10:00-15:00, Sat from 11:00; for tower-climb details, see page 121).

The church tower has a carillon that chimes every 15 minutes. At other times, it plays full songs. Invented by Dutch bellmakers in the 1400s, a carillon is a set of bells of different sizes and pitches. There's a live musician inside the tower who plays a keyboard to make the music. Mozart, Vivaldi, and Bach—all of whom lived during the heyday of the carillon—wrote music that sounds great on this unique instrument. During World War II, the Westerkerk's carillon played every day. This hopeful sound reminded Anne Frank that there was, indeed, an outside world.

▸ *Continue around the church, and walk north along the canal, past the long line of tourists marking the entrance to the ever-popular...*

⑩ Anne Frank House

This was where the Frank family hid from the Nazis for 25 months. With actual artifacts, the museum gives the cold, mind-boggling statistics of fascism the all-important intimacy of a young girl who lived through it and died from it. Even bah-humbug types find themselves caught up in Anne's story. (✪ See the Anne Frank House Tour chapter.)

▸ *At the next bridge turn left. Stop at its summit, mid-canal, for a view of...*

⑪ Prinsengracht

The "Princes' Canal" runs through one of the most livable areas in town. It's lined with houseboats, some of the city's estimated 2,500. These small vessels were once cargo ships—but by the 1930s, they had become obsolete.

They found a new use as houseboats lining the canals of Amsterdam, where dry land is so limited and pricey.

Today, former cargo holds are fashioned into elegant, cozy living rooms. The once-powerful engines have generally been removed to make more room for living space. Moorage spots are prized and grandfathered in, making some of the junky old boats worth more than you'd think. Houseboaters can plug hoses and cables into outlets along the canals to get water and electricity.

A statue to Anne Frank remembers those who hid from the Nazis in the back of a nearby house.

Notice the canal traffic. The official speed limit is about four miles per hour. At night, boats must have running lights on the top, the side, and the stern. Most boats are small and low, designed to glide under the city's bridges. The Prinsengracht bridge is average height, with less than seven feet of headroom (it varies with the water level); some bridges have less than six feet. Boaters need good charts to tell them the height, which is crucial for navigating. Police boats roam on the lookout for anyone CUI (cruising under the influence).

▸ *The recommended Café 't Smalle—though not visible from here—is nearby (see page 150). Once you cross Prinsengracht, you enter what's officially considered the Jordaan neighborhood. Facing west (toward Café de Prins), cross the bridge and veer left down...*

⓬ Nieuwe Leliestraat

Welcome to the quiet Jordaan. Built in the 1600s as a working-class housing area, it's now home to artists and yuppies. The name Jordaan probably was not derived from the French *jardin*—but given the neighborhood's garden-like ambience, it seems like it should have been.

Have your ultra-sharp "traveler's eyes" trained on all the tiny details of Amsterdam life.

Notice how the pragmatic Dutch deal with junk mail. On the doors, stickers next to mail slots say *Nee* or *Ja* (no or yes), telling the postman if they'll accept or refuse junk mail. Residents are allowed a "front-yard garden" as long as it's no more than one sidewalk tile wide. The red metal bollards known as *Amsterdammertjes* ("little Amsterdammers") have been bashing balls since the 1970s, when they were put in to stop people from parking on the sidewalks. Though many apartments have windows right on the street, the neighbors don't stare and the residents don't care.

▸ *At the first intersection, turn right onto...*

⓭ Eerste Leliedwarsstraat

Pause on this tiny lane. Imagine the frustrations of home ownership here. If your house is considered "historic," you need special permission and lots of money to renovate.

On this street, you can see three different examples of renovation. At house #9, it was done cheap and dirty: a historic (but run-down) home was torn down and replaced with an inexpensive, functional building with modern heating and plumbing. At #5, there's no renovation at all. The owners

were too poor (stuck with rent-control tenants), and they missed the window of time when a cheap rebuild was allowed. At #2A (across the street), the owners obviously had the cash to do a first-class sprucing up—it's historic-looking but fully modern inside. Even newly renovated homes must preserve their funky leaning angles and original wooden beams. They're certainly nice to look at, but absolutely maddening for owners who don't have a lot of money to meet city standards.

▸ *Just ahead, walk out to the middle of the bridge over the next canal (Egelantiersgracht). This is what I think of as...*

⓮ The Heart of the Jordaan

For me, this bridge and its surroundings capture the essence of the Jordaan. Take it all in: the bookstores, art galleries, working artists' studios, and small cafés full of rickety tables. The quiet canal is lined with trees and old, narrow buildings with gables—classic Amsterdam.

Looking south toward the Westerkerk, you'll see a completely different view of the church than most tourists get. Framed by narrow streets, crossed with streetlamp wires, and looming over shoppers on bicycles—to me, this is the church in its best light.

Turning around and looking north, the street called Tweede Egelantiersdwarsstraat is the laid-back Jordaan neighborhood's main shopping-and-people street. If you venture down there, you'll find boutiques, galleries, antique stores, hair salons, restaurants, and cafés.

▸ *Now head west along the canal (Egelantiersgracht) to the next bridge, where you'll turn left onto Tweede Leliedwarsstraat, and walk a few steps to #5.*

Some residents live on houseboats.

Want junk mail? Tell the postman no or yes.

⑮ Electric Ladyland and Other Sights

Electric Ladyland: This small shop, with a flowery window display, calls itself "The First Museum of Fluorescent Art." Its funky facade hides an illuminated wonderland within, with a tiny exhibit of black-light art. Nick Padalino—one cool cat who really found his niche in life—enjoys personally demonstrating the fluorescence found in unexpected places, from minerals to stamps to candy to the tattoo on his arm. Wow. (€5, Tue-Sat 13:30-18:00, closed Sun-Mon).

About 100 yards farther down the street is the **Paradox Coffeeshop,** a friendly, mellow place for the nervous American who wants to go local (see page 173).

▸ *To reach our last stop, backtrack 20 paces to the canal and turn left, then walk a few dozen yards to Egelantiersgracht #107, the entrance to...*

⑯ St. Andrew's Courtyard (Sint-Andrieshof)

The black door is marked *Sint-Andrieshof 107 t/m 145*. The doorway looks private, but it's the public entrance to a set of residences. It's generally

Nick welcomes you to his blacklight museum.

St. Andrew's Courtyard—low-key doorway into this quiet slice of the Jordaan

Jordaan's greatest sight: everyday life

open during daytime hours, except on Sundays. Enter quietly; you may have to push hard on the door. Go inside and continue on into a tiny garden courtyard *(hof)* surrounded by a dozen or so homes. Take a seat on a bench. This is one of the city's scores of similar *hofjes*—subsidized residences built around a courtyard, and funded by churches, charities, and the city for low-income widows and pensioners. This one, from 1613, is one of the oldest in Amsterdam.

And this is where our tour ends—in a tranquil world that seems right out of a painting by Vermeer. You're just blocks from the bustle of Amsterdam, but it feels like another world. You're immersed in the Jordaan, where everything's in its place, and life seems very good.

Anne Frank House Tour

On May 10, 1940, Germany's Luftwaffe began bombing Schiphol Airport, preparing to invade the Netherlands. The Dutch army fought back, and the Nazis responded by leveling Rotterdam. Within a week, the Netherlands surrendered, Queen Wilhelmina fled to Britain, and Nazi soldiers goose-stepped past the Westerkerk and into Dam Square, where they draped huge swastikas on the Royal Palace. A five-year occupation began.

The Anne Frank House immerses you, in a very immediate way, in the struggles and pains of the war years. Walk through rooms where, for two years, eight Amsterdam Jews hid from Nazi persecution. Though they were eventually discovered, and all but one died in concentration camps, their story has an uplifting twist—the diary of Anne Frank, an affirmation of the human spirit that cannot be crushed.

ORIENTATION

Cost: €9 in person, €9.50 online.

Hours: April-Oct daily 9:00-22:00, Nov-March daily 9:00-19:00, Sat until 21:00. Open every day except Yom Kippur.

Information: Tel. 020/556-7100, www.annefrank.org.

Getting Tickets: The Anne Frank House is extremely popular, and getting tickets takes planning. From 9:00 to 15:30, entry is only by advance reservation. After 15:30, you can purchase tickets on-site for same-day entry—but from May to September, the lines for these tickets are extremely long; it's smart to get a reservation.

Online timed-entry tickets go on sale exactly two months in advance (for example, to visit on Aug 15, you should buy online June 15). Tickets are released between 8:00-10:00 Dutch time and sell out quickly.

Museumkaart holders get in free but must reserve an entry time online for €0.50. You can make this reservation online even if you haven't purchased a pass yet, but like a ticket, you should to book it exactly two months in advance.

If you don't have an advance reservation, you can join the queue to buy a ticket and enter after 15:30. From May to September, it's smart to go at 19:00, when lines tend to be shorter.

Getting There: It's at Prinsengracht 267, near Westerkerk and about a 20-minute walk from Centraal station. You can also take tram #13, #14, or #17—or bus #170, #172 or #174—to the Westermarkt stop, about a block south of the museum's entrance.

Length of This Tour: Allow one hour.

Baggage Check: Large bags are not allowed, and there's no baggage check available (small bags are OK).

Eating: The $$ museum café serves simple fare and has good views (daily 9:30-18:00). For more suggestions, see page 150.

THE TOUR BEGINS

We'll walk through the rooms where Anne Frank's family and four other Jews hid for 25 months. The front half of the building, facing the canal, remained the offices and warehouses of an operating business. The back half, where the Franks and others lived, was the Secret Annex, its entrance concealed by a bookcase.

▸ *After the ticket desk, enter the ground-floor exhibit. After viewing the important five-minute video and a few ground-floor rooms, go upstairs to the offices of Otto Frank's business.*

First Floor: Offices

From these rooms, Otto Frank ran a successful business called Opekta, selling spices and pectin for making jelly. When the Nazis gained

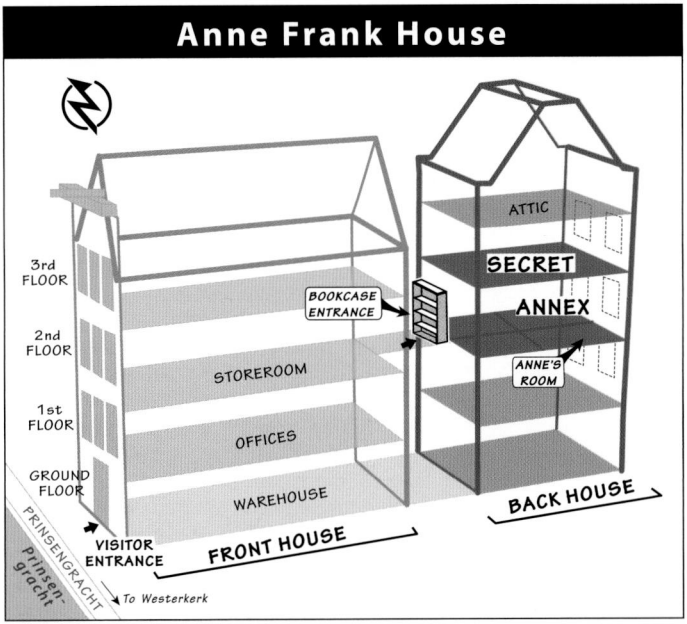

Otto Frank—Anne's father

Miep and Jan Gies helped the Franks hide.

power in Germany in 1933, Otto moved his family from Frankfurt to tolerant Amsterdam, hoping for a better life.

Photos and displays bring to life the business concerns of Otto and his colleagues. During the Nazi occupation, while the Frank family hid in the back of the building, these brave people kept Otto's business running, secretly bringing supplies to the Franks. Miep Gies, Otto's secretary (see her in the video), brought food every few days, while bookkeeper Victor Kugler cheered up Anne with the latest movie magazines.

▸ *Go upstairs to the...*

Second Floor: Storeroom

Models show the two floors where Anne, her family, and four others lived. Dollhouse furniture helps you envision the now-bare living quarters. All told, eight people lived in a tiny apartment smaller than 1,000 square feet.

At first the Nazi overlords were lenient toward, even friendly with, the vanquished Dutch. But soon they began imposing restrictions that affected one in ten Amsterdammers—that is, Jews. Jews had to wear yellow-star patches and register with the police. They were banned from movie theaters and trams, and even forbidden to ride bikes.

In February 1941, the Nazis started rounding up Amsterdam's Jews, shipping them by train to "work camps," which, in reality, were transit stations on the way to death camps in the east. Outraged, the people of Amsterdam called a general strike that shut down the city for two days... but the Nazis responded with even harsher laws.

In July 1942, Anne's sister, Margot, got her **call-up notice** for a "work-force project." Otto handed over the keys to the business to his "Aryan" colleagues, sent a final postcard to relatives, gave the family cat

to a neighbor, spread rumors that they were fleeing to Switzerland, and prepared his family to "dive under" (*onderduik,* as it was called) into hiding.

Photos put faces on the eight inhabitants of the Secret Annex. First was the Frank family—Otto and Edith and their daughters, 13-year-old Anne and 16-year-old Margot. A week later, they were joined by the Van Pels (called the "Van Daans" in her diary), with their teenage son, Peter. A few months later, Fritz Pfeffer (called "Mr. Dussel" in the diary) was invited in.

▸ *It's now time to enter the hiding place. At the back of the second floor storeroom is the clever hidden passageway into the Secret Annex.*

SECRET ANNEX

Though its furniture was ransacked during the arrest, the rooms of the annex remained virtually untouched, and we see them today much as they were.

The Bookcase Entrance

On a rainy Monday morning, July 6, 1942, the Frank family—wearing extra clothes to avoid carrying suspicious suitcases—breathed their last fresh air, took a long look at the Prinsengracht canal, and disappeared into the

This bookcase swung open to reveal a hidden passageway into the Secret Annex.

back part of the building, where they spent the next two years. Victor Kugler concealed the entrance to the annex with this swinging bookcase, stacked with business files.

Though not exactly a secret (since it's hard to hide an entire building), the annex was a typical back house *(achterhuis),* a common feature in Amsterdam buildings, and the Nazis had no reason to suspect anything on the premises of the legitimate Opekta business.

▸ *Pass through the bookcase entrance into...*

Otto, Edith, and Margot's Room

The family carried on life as usual. Edith read from a **prayer book** in their native German, Otto read Dickens' ***Sketches by Boz,*** and the children continued their studies, with Margot taking **Latin lessons** by correspondence course. They avidly followed the course of the war by radio broadcasts and news from their helpers. As the tides of war slowly turned and it appeared they might one day be saved from the Nazis, Otto tracked the Allied advance on a **map** of Normandy.

The room is very small, even without the furniture. Imagine yourself and two fellow tourists confined here for two years.

Pencil lines on the wall track Margot's and Anne's heights, marking the point at which these growing lives were cut short.

Anne Frank's Room

Pan the room clockwise to see some of the young girl's idols in photos and clippings she pasted there herself: American stars Robert Stack and Deanna Durbin from the Cinderella-story film *First Love,* the future Queen Elizabeth II as a child, matinee idol Rudy Vallee, figure-skating actress Sonja Henie, and, on the other wall, actress Greta Garbo, actor Ray Milland, Renaissance man Leonardo da Vinci, and actress Ginger Rogers. Photos of flowers and landscapes gave Anne a window on the outside world she was forbidden to see.

Out the window (which had to be blacked out) is the back courtyard, which had a chestnut tree and a few buildings. (In 2010, the tree, which Anne had greatly enjoyed, toppled in a storm.) These things, along with the Westerkerk bell chiming every 15 minutes, represented the borders of Anne's "outside world." Imagine Anne sitting here at a small desk, writing in her diary.

In November 1942, the Franks invited a Jewish neighbor to join them,

Life in the Annex

By day, it's enforced silence, so no one can hear them in the offices. They whisper, tiptoe, and step around squeaky places in the floor. The windows are blacked out, so they can't even look outside. They read or study, and Anne writes in her diary.

At night and on weekends, when the offices close, one or two might sneak downstairs to listen to Winston Churchill's BBC broadcasts on the office radio. Everyone's spirits rise and sink with news of Allied victories and setbacks.

Anne's diaries make clear the tensions, petty quarrels, and domestic politics of eight people living under intense pressure. Mr. Van Pels annoys Anne, but he gets along well with Margot. Anne never gets used to Mr. Pfeffer, who is literally invading her space. Most troublesome of all, pubescent Anne often strikes sparks with her mom. (Anne's angriest comments about her mother were deleted from early editions of the published diary.)

Despite their hardships, the group feels guilty: They have shelter, while so many other Jews are being rounded up and sent off. As the war progresses, they endure long nights when the house shakes from Allied air raids, and Anne cuddles up in her dad's bed.

Boredom tinged with fear—this existentialist hell is captured so well in Anne's journal.

and Anne was forced to share the tiny room with Fritz Pfeffer, a middle-aged dentist.

The Bathroom

The eight inhabitants shared this bathroom. During the day, they didn't dare flush the toilet.

Anne Frank House: Secret Annex

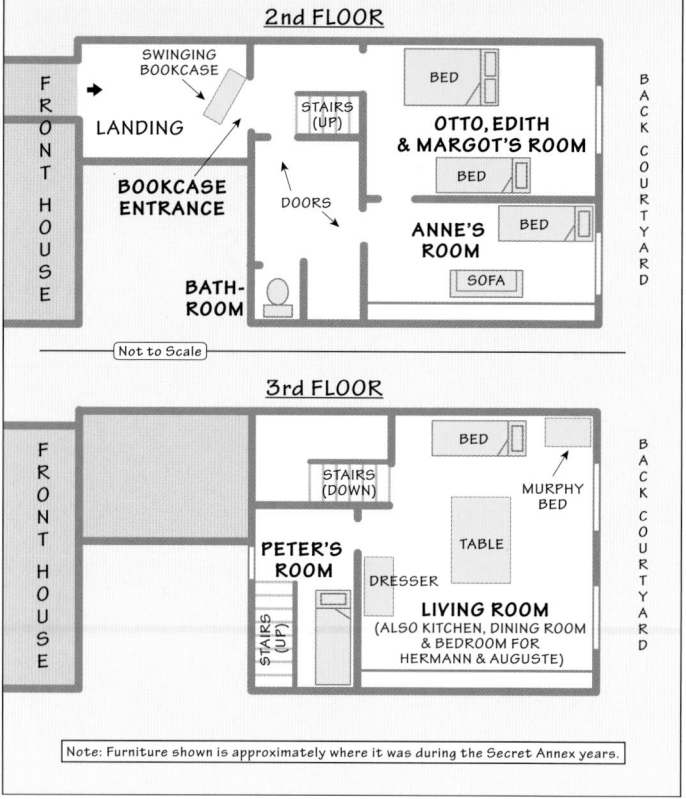

▸ *Ascend the steep staircase—silently—to the...*

Common Living Room

This was the kitchen (note the remains of the stove and sink) and dining room. Otto Frank was well off, and early on, the annex was well-stocked with food. Miep Gies would dutifully take their shopping list, buy food for her "family" of eight, and secretly lug it up to them. Buying such large quantities in a coupon-rationed economy was highly suspect, but she knew a sympathetic grocer (a block away on Leliegracht) who was part of a ring of Amsterdammers risking their lives to help the Jews.

The **menu** for a special dinner lists soup, roast beef, salad, potatoes, rice, dessert, and coffee. Later, as war and German restrictions plunged Holland into poverty and famine, they survived on canned foods and dried kidney beans.

The inhabitants spent their days reading and studying in this room. At night, it became sleeping quarters for Hermann and Auguste van Pels.

Peter van Pels' Room

On Peter's 16th birthday, he got a Monopoly-like board game called "The Broker" as a present.

Initially, Anne was cool toward Peter, but after two years together, a courtship developed, and their flirtation culminated in a kiss.

The **staircase** (no visitor access) leads up to where the inhabitants stored their food. Anne loved to steal away here for a bit of privacy. At night they'd open a hatch to let in fresh air.

One hot August day, Otto was in this room helping Peter learn English, when they looked up to see a man with a gun. The hiding was over.

▸ *From here we leave the Secret Annex, returning to the Opekta storeroom and offices in the front house. As you work your way downstairs, you'll see a number of exhibits on the aftermath of this story.*

AFTERMATH

Arrest, Deportation, and Auschwitz Exhibits

On August 4, 1944, a German policeman accompanied by three Dutch Nazis pulled up in a car, politely entered the Opekta office, and went straight to the bookcase entrance. No one knows who tipped them off. The police

gave the surprised hiders time to pack. They demanded their valuables and stuffed them into Anne's briefcase...after dumping her diaries onto the floor.

Taken in a van to Gestapo headquarters, the eight were processed in an efficient, bureaucratic manner, then placed on a train to Westerbork, a concentration camp northeast of the city (you'll see the **transport list,** which includes "Anneliese Frank," and their 3-by-5-inch **registration cards**).

From there they were locked in a car on a normal passenger train and sent to Auschwitz, a Nazi extermination camp in Poland. On the platform at Auschwitz, they were "forcibly separated from each other" (as Otto later reported) and sent to different camps. Anne and Margot were sent to Bergen-Belsen.

Don't miss the **video** of one of Anne's former neighbors, Hannah Goslar, who, by chance, ended up at Bergen-Belsen with Anne. In English she describes their reunion as they talked through a barbed-wire fence shortly before Anne died. She says of Anne, "She didn't have any more tears."

Anne and Margot both died of typhus in March 1945, only weeks before the camp was liberated. The other Secret Annex residents—except Otto—were gassed or died of disease.

The Franks' story was that of Holland's Jews. The seven who died were among the more than 100,000 Dutch Jews killed during the war years. (Before the war, 135,000 Jews lived in the Netherlands.) Of Anne's school class of 87 Jews, only 20 survived.

▸ *The next room is devoted to Anne's father.*

The Otto Frank Room

After the war, Otto returned to Amsterdam. Miep Gies had a gift for him—Anne's diaries, which she had found on the floor of the annex after the arrest. Listen to a 1967 video, in which Anne's father talks about his reaction as he read the diaries. He was struck by the enormous power of Anne's ideas and emotions—a secret world he'd never known inside his daughter. Determined to make her writings available to a wider audience, he set about contacting publishers (you may see his letters or notebooks or early typed-up drafts of the diaries). In 1947, the diaries were first published in Dutch as *De Achterhuis*—"The Back House."

▸ *Downstairs you come to...*

The Diaries

Anne wrote three different diaries. (You may see one, two, or all three of

them, as well as individual pages.) She received the first diary (with a red-plaid binding) as a birthday present when she turned 13, shortly before the family went into hiding. The other two were written in school-exercise books. Anne wrote the diaries in the form of a letter to an imaginary friend named Kitty. As she wrote more and more, Anne began to recognize the uniqueness of her situation. You may see some loose-leaf pages on which she reworked parts of her diary. You may also see a book of Anne's short stories and a notebook she kept of favorite quotes.

When the diaries were published, the book quickly when viral. *De Achterhuis* in Dutch soon became *The Diary of a Young Girl* in English (1952), followed by translations in many other languages. The book became a popular play, *The Diary of Anne Frank,* and then a Hollywood movie.

▸ *Continue downstairs to the ground-floor exhibits.*

Anne's Legacy

These displays (which change often) capture the Anne Frank legacy. You may see video interviews of people who knew Anne, such as childhood friends or Miep Gies (who passed away in 2010 at the age of 100). You

Anne's diaries chronicled both her tedious life in hiding and her expansive dreams.

may learn about Otto's struggles to save the house from demolition and turn it into a museum.

The displays do not try to sum up "the moral" of the story. Instead, they recognize that World War II presented many gray areas and ethical dilemmas, and different people had different responses. The point? To keep visitors from leaving the museum with pat feelings of easy moral clarity.

The Anne Frank Foundation is obviously concerned that we learn from Europe's Nazi nightmare. The thinking that made the Holocaust possible still survives. Even today, some groups promote the notion that the Holocaust never occurred and contend that stories like Anne Frank's are only a hoax. It was Otto Frank's dream that visitors come away from the Anne Frank House with hope for a better world. He wrote: "The task that Anne entrusted to me continually gives me new strength to strive for reconciliation and for human rights all over the world."

Anne's much-read diary has helped turn the Franks' personal struggle into a universal story.

Sights in Amsterdam

One of Amsterdam's delights is that it has perhaps more specialty museums than any other city its size. From houseboats to sex, from marijuana to Old Masters, you can find a museum to suit your interests.

The following sights are arranged by neighborhood for handy sightseeing. When you see a ✪ in a listing, it means the sight is covered in much more depth in one of my walks or self-guided tours.

A few quick tips: Avoid long ticket lines at the Anne Frank House, Van Gogh Museum, and Rijksmuseum by getting tickets in advance (see page 167). A sightseeing pass (the Museumkaart or I Amsterdam Card) can save time and money (see page 168). Most sights have plenty of English explanations. For canal boat tours, see page 173. Finally, remember that though the city has several must-see museums, its best attraction is its own carefree ambience.

Amsterdam Sights

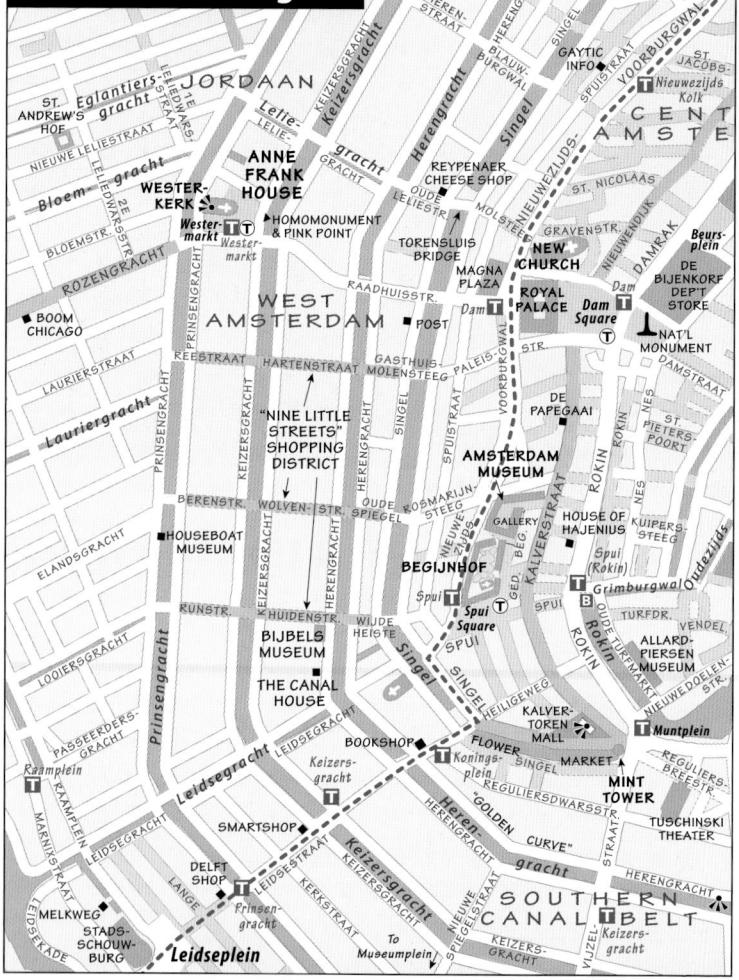

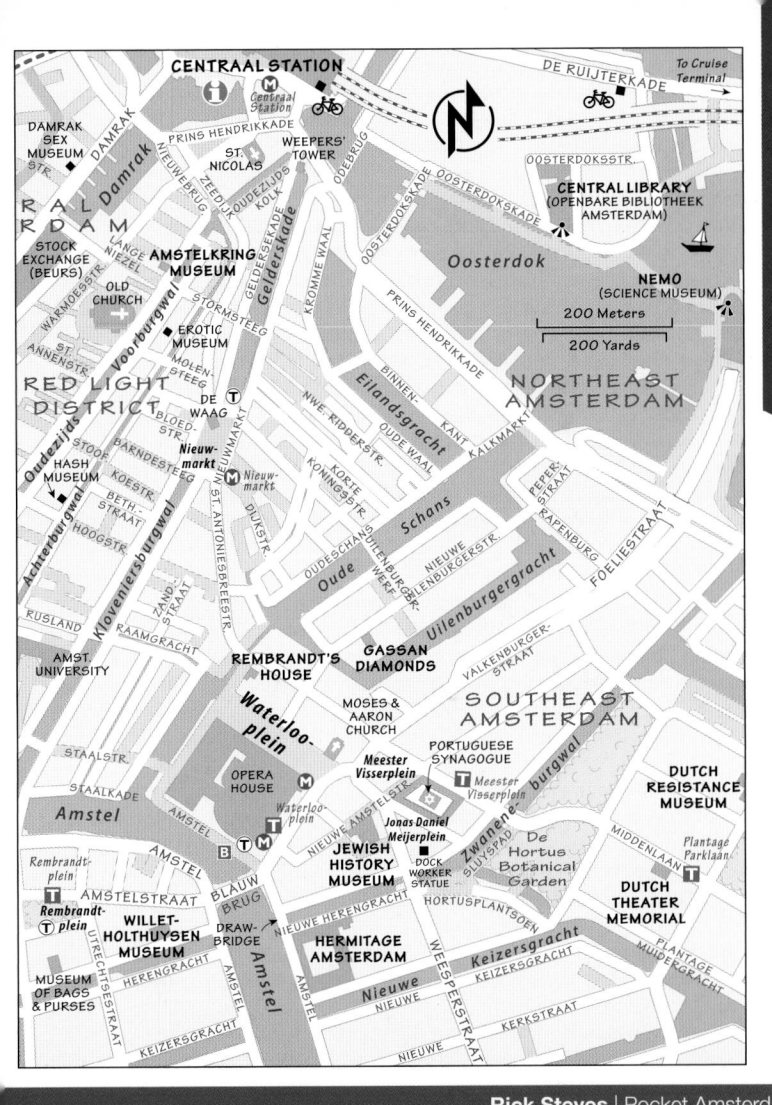
CENTRAAL STATION
Centraal Station
DE RUIJTERKADE
To Cruise Terminal
DAMRAK SEX MUSEUM
DAMRAK STR.
PRINS HENDRIKKADE
WEEPERS' TOWER
ST. NICOLAS
NIEUWEBRUG
ZEEDIJK
OUDEZIJDS KOLK
OOSTERDOKSSTR.
OOSTERDOKSKADE
DE OOSTERDOKSKADE
CENTRAL LIBRARY (OPENBARE BIBLIOTHEEK AMSTERDAM)
Damrak
Gelderskade
GELDERSEKADE
STOCK EXCHANGE (BEURS)
LANGE NIEZEL
AMSTELKRING MUSEUM
OLD CHURCH
WARMOESSTR.
STORMSTEEG
Oosterdok
NEMO (SCIENCE MUSEUM)
200 Meters
200 Yards
EROTIC MUSEUM
Voorburgwal
ST. ANNENSTR.
MOLEN-STEEG
KROMME WAAL
PRINS HENDRIKKADE
RED LIGHT DISTRICT
DE WAAG
BLOED-STR.
BINNEN-KANT
Eilandsgracht
NORTHEAST AMSTERDAM
NIEUWMARKT
NWE RIJDERSTR.
OUDE WAAL
KALKMARKT
Oudezijds
STOOF
BARNDESTEEG
Nieuwmarkt
Nieuwmarkt
HASH MUSEUM
KONINGSSTR.
KORTE KONINGSSTR.
PEPERSTRAAT
KOESTR.
BETH-STRAAT
ST. ANTONIESBREESTR.
DUKSTR.
Schans
KAFENBURG
Achterburgwal
HOOGSTR.
OUDE SCHANS
UILENBURGERWERF
NIEUWE UILENBURGERSTR.
FOELIESTRAAT
Oude
Uilenburgergracht
Kloveniersburgwal
TANDSTRAAT
RUSLAND
RAAMGRACHT
AMST. UNIVERSITY
REMBRANDT'S HOUSE
GASSAN DIAMONDS
VALKENBURGERSTRAAT
Waterloo-plein
MOSES & AARON CHURCH
SOUTHEAST AMSTERDAM
PORTUGUESE SYNAGOGUE
Meester Visserplein
Meester Visserplein
STAALSTR.
STAALKADE
OPERA HOUSE
Waterloo-plein
DUTCH RESISTANCE MUSEUM
Amstel
AMSTEL
NIEUWE AMSTELSTR.
Jonas Daniel Meijerplein
Zwanenburgwal
SLUISPAD
De Hortus Botanical Garden
MIDDENLAAN
Plantage Parklaan
Rembrandt-plein
AMSTEL
JEWISH HISTORY MUSEUM
DOCK WORKER STATUE
AMSTELSTRAAT
BLAUW BRUG
NIEUWE HERENGRACHT
HORTUSPLANTSOEN
DUTCH THEATER MEMORIAL
Rembrandt-plein
WILLET-HOLTHUYSEN MUSEUM
DRAW-BRIDGE
HERMITAGE AMSTERDAM
Keizersgracht
KEIZERSGRACHT
PLANTAGE MUIDERGRACHT
MUSEUM OF BAGS & PURSES
HERENGRACHT
UTRECHTSESTRAAT
Amstel
AMSTEL
Nieuwe
NIEUWE
WEESPERSTRAAT
KERKSTRAAT
KEIZERSGRACHT
NIEUWE

Central Amsterdam

The historic center extends from Centraal station to the Mint Tower—the area enclosed by the Singel canal. The following sights are all either on or within a 10-minute walk of Dam Square.

▲Royal Palace (Koninklijk Huis)

Built as a lavish City Hall (1648-1655)—when Amsterdam was the richest city on the planet, awash in profit from trade—this building became a "Royal Palace" when Napoleon installed his brother Louis as king (1806). The Dutch royal family (the House of Orange) lived here, and current King Willem-Alexander numbers it among his official residences. About 20 of the palace's lavishly decorated rooms are open to the public.

The highlight is the vast, white Citizens' Hall—120 feet by 60 feet by 90 feet, and lit by eight big chandeliers. At the far end, a statue of Atlas holds the globe of the world, and the ceiling painting shows Lady Amsterdam triumphant amid the clouds of heaven. On the floor, inlaid maps show the known world circa 1750 (back when the West Coast of the US was still being explored). The hall is used today for hosting foreign dignitaries and for royal family wedding receptions.

You'll see the room where Louis Bonaparte's throne once sat (in front of the fireplace), a room of impressive Empire Style furniture (high-polished wood with Neoclassical motifs), and the childhood bedroom of former Queen Beatrix. The palace's rich chandeliers, paintings, statues, and furniture reflect Amsterdam's historic status as the center of global trade.

▸ *€10, includes audioguide, daily 10:00-17:00 but hours can vary for official business—check website, tel. 020/620-4060, www.paleisamsterdam.nl.*

New Church (Nieuwe Kerk)

Barely newer than the Red Light District's "Old" Church, this 15th-century sanctuary has a spare interior, lots of tradition (royal weddings and coronations), and popular temporary exhibits.

✪ See page 23 of the Amsterdam City Walk chapter.

▲Begijnhof

Stepping into this tiny, idyllic courtyard in the city center, you escape into the charm of old Amsterdam.

✪ See page 27 of the Amsterdam City Walk chapter.

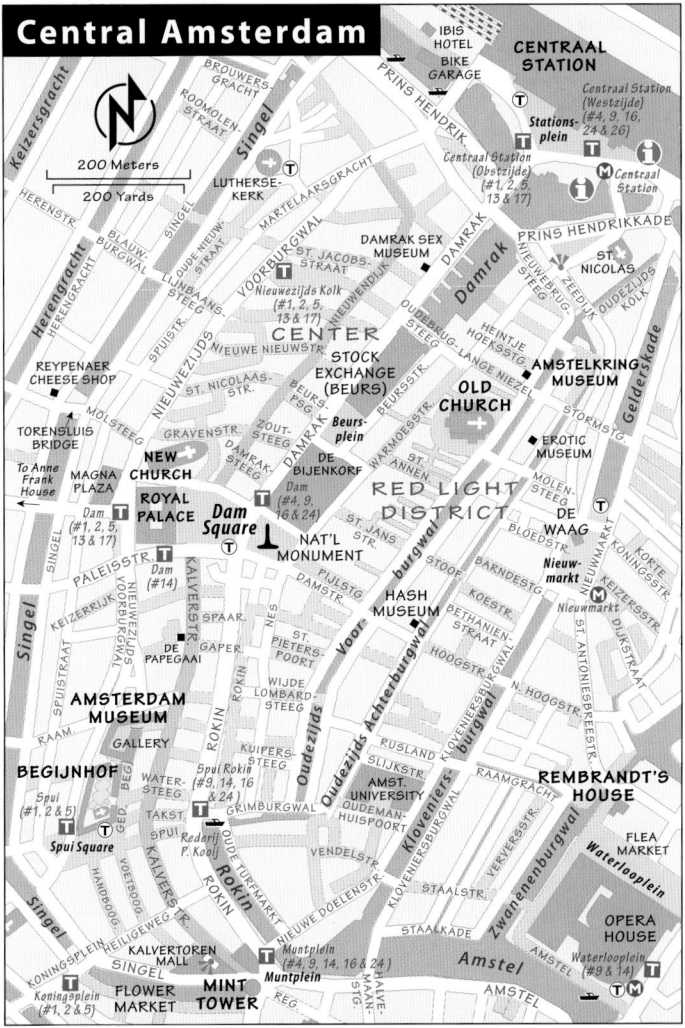
Central Amsterdam
200 Meters
200 Yards
IBIS HOTEL
BIKE GARAGE
CENTRAAL STATION
Centraal Station (Westzijde) (#4, 9, 16, 24 & 26)
Stations-plein
Centraal Station (Oostzijde) (#1, 2, 5, 13 & 17)
Centraal Station
PRINS HENDRIK.
PRINS HENDRIKKADE
BROUWERS-GRACHT
ROOMOLEN-STRAAT
Singel
Keizersgracht
LUTHERSE-KERK
MARTELAARSGRACHT
HEREN-STR.
BLAUW-BURGWAL
OUDE NIEUW-STRAAT
LINBANS-STEEG
Herengracht
HERENGRACHT
VOORBURGWAL
ST. JACOBS-STRAAT
DAMRAK SEX MUSEUM
DAMRAK
Damrak
NIEUWEBRUG-STEEG
ZEEDIJK
ST. NICOLAS
OUDEZIJDS KOLK
Nieuwezijds Kolk (#1, 2, 5, 13 & 17)
NIEUWENDIJK
OUDEBRUG-STEEG
HEINTJE HOEKSTG.
LANGE NIEZEL
CENTER
STOCK EXCHANGE (BEURS)
OLD CHURCH
AMSTELKRING MUSEUM
Gelderskade
NIEUWEZIJDS
SPUIST.
NIEUWE NIEUWSTR.
ST. NICOLAAS-STR.
REYPENAER CHEESE SHOP
MOLSTEEG
GRAVENSTR.
ZOUT-STEEG
BEURS-PSG.
BEURSSTR.
Beurs-plein
STORMSTG.
EROTIC MUSEUM
TORENSLUIS BRIDGE
To Anne Frank House
MAGNA PLAZA
NEW CHURCH
DAMRAK-STEEG
DE BIJENKORF
WARMOESSTR.
ST. ANNEN
Dam (#4, 9, 16 & 24)
RED LIGHT DISTRICT
MOLEN-STEEG
DE WAAG
Dam (#1, 2, 5, 13 & 17)
ROYAL PALACE
Dam Square
NAT'L MONUMENT
ST. JANS-STR.
BLOEDSTR.
Nieuwmarkt
KORTE KONINGSSTR.
SINGEL
PALEISSTR.
Dam (#14)
KALVERSTR.
PUIJSTG.
DAMSTR.
STOOF
BARNDESTG.
KOESTR.
HASH MUSEUM
Voorburgwal
KEIZERSTR.
Nieuwmarkt
KEIZERRIJK
WEUWEZIJDS VOORBURGWAL
SPAAR.
NES
BETHANIEN-STRAAT
ST. ANTONIESBREESTR.
DIJKSTRAAT
DE PAPEGAAI
GAPER.
ST. PIETERS-POORT
HOOGSTR.
KLOVENIERSBURGWAL
N. HOOGSTR.
SPUISTRAAT
WIJDE LOMBARD-STEEG
ROKIN
AMSTERDAM MUSEUM
RAAM.
GALLERY
KUIPERS-STEEG
Oudezijds Achterburgwal
Oudezijds
RUSLAND
SLIJKSTR.
BEGIJNHOF
Spui Rokin (#9, 14, 16 & 24)
WATER-STEEG
AMST. UNIVERSITY
RAAMGRACHT
REMBRANDT'S HOUSE
Spui (#1, 2 & 5)
BEG.
GED.
TAKST.
GRIMBURGWAL
OUDEMAN-HUISPOORT
Spui Square
SPUI
Rederij P. Kooij
OUDE TURFMARKT
Kloveniers-burgwal
VERVERSSTR.
FLEA MARKET
Waterlooplein
KALVERSTR.
VENDELSTR.
HANDBOOGSTR.
VOETBOOG
Rokin
KLOVENIERSBURGWAL
STAALSTR.
Zwanenburgwal
Singel
HELIGENWEG
NIEUWE DOELENSTR.
OPERA HOUSE
STAALKADE
KALVERTOREN MALL
Muntplein (#4, 9, 14, 16 & 24)
Amstel
Waterlooplein (#9 & 14)
AMSTEL
KONINGSPLEIN
Koningsplein (#1, 2 & 5)
FLOWER MARKET
MINT TOWER
Muntplein
REG.
HALVE-MAANSTG.

▲▲Amsterdam Museum

This creative museum works hard to make the city's history engaging and fun. The "DNA" section gives a quick overview. Then interactive exhibits help you follow the city's growth from fishing village to global trade center to Rembrandt (several paintings) to 1960s hippie haven, and the many challenges of the 21st century: housing, drug policy, prostitution, and immigration issues.

▸ *€12.50, includes audioguide, daily 10:00-17:00, pleasant restaurant, uncrowded place to buy Museumkaart, located next to Begijnhof at Kalverstraat 92, tel. 020/523-1822, www.ahm.nl.*

✪ *For more on the museum and its free, portrait-lined pedestrian corridor, see page 26 of the Amsterdam City Walk chapter.*

▲▲Amstelkring Museum

For two centuries (1578-1795), Catholicism in Amsterdam was illegal but tolerated (like pot in the 1970s). Catholic churches were vandalized and Catholic kids were razzed on their way to school. Catholics were forbidden to worship openly, so they gathered secretly to say Mass in homes and offices.

Imagine the jubilation in 1663 when Our Lord in the Attic opened its doors. The church—embedded within a merchant's townhouse—was low-profile enough to appease the Protestant authorities but glorious enough to inspire the Catholic faithful.

Today, at the Amstelkring Museum, you can visit the church, as well as the merchant's apartments and servants' back house. Start with the...

Merchant's Apartments: The ornate Reception Room (with a big fireplace) is where he entertained guests. In the Drawing Room (with period furnishings), the family hung out, and they slept in an upstairs bedroom, sitting upright in small bed cabinets.

The Church: The church is long and narrow, with an altar at one end, an organ at the other, and two balconies overhead to maximize the seating (150 worshippers) in this relatively small space. Compared with Amsterdam's whitewashed Protestant churches, this Catholic church has touches of elaborate Baroque decor, with statues of saints, garlands, and baby angels.

Look closely at the altar. The base of the left column—made of wood painted to look like marble—is hollow. Inside was a foldout wooden pulpit.

The Amstelkring historic house with...

...a hidden Catholic church in the attic.

If it's closed for your visit, you can at least see how it could swing out like a door.

Browse nearby rooms to see Catholic religious paraphernalia—a 400-year-old altar, a collection box *(voor St. Pieter),* a confessional, several gold monstrances—the kind of luxury, ostentation, and Catholic mumbo-jumbo that drove thrifty Calvinists nuts. Continue downstairs in...

The Back House: Like many townhomes, this had rooms at the back. You'll see a reconstructed kitchen, with blue tiles on the walls showing tiny playful scenes of kids and animals. Step into the small pantry, then open a door to see the toilet.

The Rest of the Museum: Upstairs in the new building, you'll find a small exhibit on the so-called "Miracle of Amsterdam," a window from where you can view the broad side of the hidden church, and a thoughtful corner celebrating the Dutch concept of finding community and consensus through tolerance.

▸ *€10, includes audioguide, Mon-Sat 10:00-17:00, Sun 13:00-17:00, steep staircases, Oudezijds Voorburgwal 40, tel. 020/624-6604, www.opsolder.nl.*

▲▲Red Light District

Europe's most popular ladies of the night tease and tempt here, as they have for centuries, in streets surrounding the historic Old Church (Oude Kerk). The neighborhood also boasts sex shops, a sex museum, marijuana cafes, and a marijuana museum. It's liveliest and least seedy in the evening.

✪ See the Red Light District Walk chapter.

Sex Museums

Amsterdam has three sex museums. While visiting one can be called sightseeing, visiting more is harder to explain.

The **Erotic Museum** in the Red Light District is five floors of uninspired paintings, videos, old photos, and sculpture (€7, not covered by Museumkaart, daily 11:00-24:00, at Oudezijds Achterburgwal 54, tel. 020/624-7303, www.erotisch-museum.nl. ✪ see page 82).

Red Light Secrets Museum of Prostitution is a pricey look at the world's oldest profession. If you're wondering what it's like to sit in those red booths, watch the video taken from the prostitute's perspective as "johns" check you out. (€10 in person, €8 online, not covered by Museumkaart, daily 11:00-24:00, Oudezijds Achterburgwal 60, tel. 020/662-5300, www.redlightsecrets.com).

The **Damrak Sex Museum** is cheaper and better. It tells the story of pornography from Roman times through 1960. Every sexual deviation is revealed. You'll see early French pornographic photos; memorabilia from Europe, India, and Asia; a Marilyn Monroe tribute; and some S&M displays (€4, not covered by Museumkaart, daily 9:30-23:00, Damrak 18, a block in front of Centraal station, tel. 020/622-8376).

West Amsterdam

Walking west from busy Dam Square, you quickly reach a quieter world of leafy streets along some of the city's grandest canals. Farther west is the residential Jordaan neighborhood.

▲▲▲Anne Frank House

Thirteen-year-old Anne and her family spent two years hiding in the back rooms of this townhouse during the Nazi occupation. The thoughtfully designed exhibit covers the family's ordeal, Anne's famous diary, and the Holocaust.

✪ See the Anne Frank House Tour chapter.

Houseboat Museum (Woonbootmuseum)

In the 1930s, modern cargo ships came into widespread use. The old, sail-powered cargo boats found new life as houseboats lining the canals of Amsterdam. Today, 2,500 such boats—their cargo holds turned into classy, comfortable living rooms—are called home. For a peek into this *gezellig* (cozy) world, visit this tiny museum. Captain Vincent enjoys

Houseboat Museum with Captain Vincent

The Stedelijk has wild modern art.

showing visitors around his 100-year-old houseboat, which feels lived-in because, until 1997, it was.

- *€4.50; March-Oct Tue-Sun 11:00-17:00, closed Mon; Nov-Dec and Feb Fri-Sun 11:00-17:00, closed Mon-Thu; closed most of Jan; on Prinsengracht, opposite #296 facing Elandsgracht, tel. 020/427-0750, www.houseboatmuseum.nl.*

Westerkerk

The landmark church has a barren interior, Rembrandt's body buried somewhere under the pews, and Amsterdam's tallest steeple, with a grand city view. To go up the tower, you must take a tour (limited to six people; reserve in person on same day or call).

- *Church entry—free, generally April-Sept Mon-Fri 10:00-15:00, Sat 11:00-15:00, closed Sun and Oct-March; tower—€7.50 by tour only, April-Sept Mon-Sat 10:00-20:00, closed Sun and Nov-March, tours leave on the half-hour; Prinsengracht 281, tel. 020/624-7766 www.westerkerk.nl.*

Southwest Amsterdam

Three major museums dot the landscape of the large park called Museumplein. Several other interesting sights lie nearby, as well as recommended eateries. Everything is within a 5- to 10-minute walk. Trams #2 and #5 from Centraal station drop you right there.

▲▲▲Rijksmuseum

This incomparable collection of 17th-century Dutch Masters is led by Rembrandt's brooding brown canvases, Vermeer's slice-of-life moments, Hals' vivacious portraits, and Steen's whimsical tableaux.

✪ See the Rijksmuseum Tour chapter.

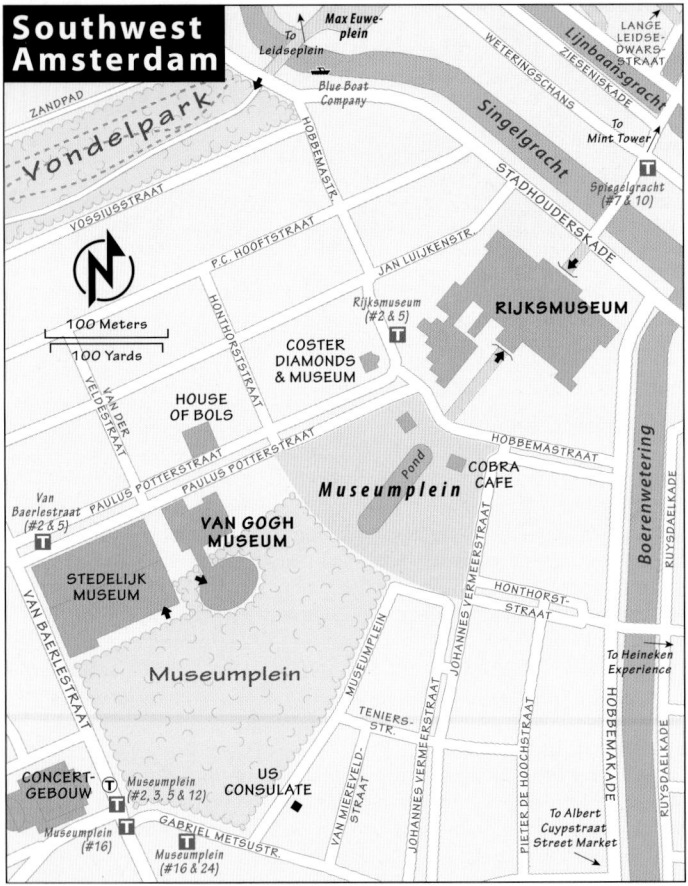
Southwest Amsterdam
To Leidseplein
Max Euwe-plein
Blue Boat Company
LANGE LEIDSE-DWARS-STRAAT
WETERINGSCHANS
ZIESENISKADE
Lijnbaansgracht
ZANDPAD
Vondelpark
HOBBEMASTR.
Singelgracht
To Mint Tower
Spiegelgracht (#7 & 10)
VOSSIUSSTRAAT
STADHOUDERSKADE
P.C. HOOFTSTRAAT
JAN LUIJKENSTR.
100 Meters
100 Yards
HONTHORSTSTRAAT
Rijksmuseum (#2 & 5)
RIJKSMUSEUM
COSTER DIAMONDS & MUSEUM
VAN DER VELDESTRAAT
HOUSE OF BOLS
HOBBEMASTRAAT
PAULUS POTTERSTRAAT
Pond
COBRA CAFE
Museumplein
Van Baerlestraat (#2 & 5)
VAN GOGH MUSEUM
Boerenwetering
RUYSDAELKADE
STEDELIJK MUSEUM
JOHANNES VERMEERSTRAAT
HONTHORST-STRAAT
VAN BAERLESTRAAT
MUSEUMPLEIN
To Heineken Experience
Museumplein
TENIERS-STR.
HOBBEMAKADE
CONCERT-GEBOUW
Museumplein (#2, 3, 5 & 12)
US CONSULATE
VAN WIEREVELD-STRAAT
PIETER DE HOOCHSTRAAT
To Albert Cuypstraat Street Market
Museumplein (#16)
GABRIEL METSUSTR.
Museumplein (#16 & 24)

▲▲▲Van Gogh Museum

The museum's 200 paintings offer a virtual stroll through the artist's work and life. Highlights include *Sunflowers, The Bedroom, The Potato Eaters,* and many brooding self-portraits.

✪ See the Van Gogh Museum Tour chapter.

▲▲Stedelijk Museum

The Netherlands' top modern-art museum is fun, far-out, and refreshing. The collection includes post-1945 experimental and conceptual art as well as works by Picasso, Chagall, and many more, but be sure to pay special attention to the many Dutch artists who helped to create modern art. The Stedelijk (STAYD-eh-lik) boasts a newly spiffed-up building, which flaunts an architecturally daring entry aptly nicknamed "the bathtub."

▸ *€15, daily 10:00-18:00, Fri until 22:00, top-notch gift shop, restaurant with outdoor seating, Paulus Potterstraat 13 tel. 020/573-2911, www.stedelijk.nl.*

▲Museumplein

This park-like square bordered by the Rijks, Van Gogh, Stedelijk, and the Concertgebouw (classical music hall) is interesting even to art haters. Amsterdam's best acoustics are found underneath the Rijksmuseum, where street musicians perform everything from chamber music to Mongolian throat singing. Mimes, human statues, and crafts booths dot the square. Skateboarders careen across a concrete tube, while locals enjoy a park bench or a coffee at the Cobra Café.

Nearby is **Coster Diamonds,** a handy place to see a diamond-cutting and polishing demo (free, frequent, and interesting 30-minute

Museumplein—a people-friendly park

Heineken brewery—a frothy "experience"

tours followed by sales pitch, daily 9:00-17:00, Paulus Potterstraat 2-6, tel. 020/305-5555, www.costerdiamonds.com). Their Diamond Museum is worthwhile for those who have a Museumkaart or feel the need to see more diamonds (€8.50, covered by Museumkaart, daily 9:00-17:00, tel. 020/305-5300, www.diamantmuseumamsterdam.nl).

The **House of Bols: Cocktail & Genever Experience** is a fun self-guided walk through what is essentially an ad for Holland's leading distillery, culminating in a chance to taste local gins (€15, not covered by Museumkaart, daily 13:00-18:30, Fri-Sat until 21:00, last entry one hour before closing, must be 18, Paulus Potterstraat 14, tel. 020/570-8575, www.houseofbols.com).

Heineken Experience

This famous brewery, having moved its operations to the suburbs, has converted its original headquarters into a slick, Disneyesque beerfest. There's a beer-making simulation ride, do-it-yourself music videos, wacky photo ops, and lots of hype about all things Heineken. It's fun, if overpriced.

- *€18 in person, €16 online, includes two drinks, daily 10:30-19:30, Fri-Sun until 21:00, last entry 2 hours before closing; tram #16, #24, or #25 to Stadhouderskade; an easy walk from Rijksmuseum, Stadhouderskade 78, tel. 020/523-9222, www.heinekenexperience.com.*

▲▲Vondelpark

This huge, lively city park is popular with families, romantic couples, strolling seniors, and hipsters sharing blankets and beers. It's a favored venue

Vondelpark—paths, greenery, happy locals

Willet-Holthuysen—a historic mansion

The Netherlands

The word *Netherlands* means "lowlands." ("Holland" is just a nickname; North and South Holland are two of the country's 12 provinces.) The country occupies the low-lying delta near the mouth of three of Europe's large rivers, including the Rhine. In medieval times, inhabitants built a system of earthen dikes to protect their land from flooding caused by tides and storm surges. Today's 350 miles of dikes and levees are high-tech. Much of the Dutch landscape is reclaimed from the sea, rivers, and lakes.

The Netherlands is Europe's most densely populated country (16.7 million people, 1,200 people per square mile), and the average income is on a par with the US ($42,700). Though only 8 percent of the labor force is made up of farmers, 70 percent of the land is cultivated.

Several Dutch icons came directly from the country's flat, reclaimed landscape: Windmills and canals drained the land. Wooden shoes *(klompen)* allowed farmers to walk across soggy fields. Tulips and other flowers grew well in the sandy soil near dunes. All this technological tinkering with nature prompted a popular local saying: "God made the Earth, but the Dutch made Holland."

for free summer concerts. On a sunny afternoon, it's a hedonistic scene that seems to say, "Parents...relax."

Southern Canal Belt

This outer ring of canals lies south (and southwest) of the Old Center. The neighborhood's broad canals and classically gabled townhouses make it a pleasant and quiet area, speckled with a few small sights.

▲Leidseplein

Brimming with cafés, this people-watching mecca is an impromptu stage for street artists, jugglers, and unicyclists. At night, it hums.

✪ For more on Leidseplein, see page 33 of the Amsterdam City Walk.

Rembrandtplein and Tuschinski Theater

One of the city's premier nightlife spots is the leafy Rembrandtplein (and

the adjoining Thorbeckeplein). On the square stands a fun 3-D statue group recreating Rembrandt's *The Night Watch.* The nearby **Tuschinski Theater,** a movie palace from the 1920s (a half-block from Rembrandtplein at Reguliersbreestraat 26-28), glitters inside and out. The exterior design forces the round peg of Art Nouveau (Tiffany-style windows, curvy iron lamps) into the square hole of Art Deco. Inside, the lobby (free to enter) is sumptuous. The Tuschinski is a delightful old place to see first-run movies.

▸ *€10 for half-hour tour, daily 9:00-11:30, trams #4, #9, and #14 go to Rembrandtplein.*

▲Willet-Holthuysen Museum (a.k.a. Herengracht Canal Mansion)

This 1687 townhouse is a must for devotees of Hummel-topped sugar bowls and Louis XVI-style wainscoting. For others, it's a pleasant look inside a typical (rich) home with much of the original furniture and decor. Forget the history and just browse through a dozen rooms of beautiful saccharine objects from the 19th century.

A ground-floor video explains how the wealthy heiress Louise Holthuysen and the art-collecting bon vivant Abraham Willet got married and became joined at the hyphen, then set out to make their home the social hub of Amsterdam.

You'll see their pre-electricity kitchen, their paintings of frolicking French nobles, and rooms of Louis XVI-style furniture. Imagine Abraham and Louise entertaining in the impressive gilded ballroom, then retiring to the dining room to eat off the 275-piece Meissen porcelain set, and finishing with tea in the conservatory, gazing out at symmetrically curved hedges and classical statues. You'll even see the couple's bedroom, with a canopy bed and a chamber pot tucked beneath.

▸ *€8, Mon-Fri 10:00-17:00, Sat-Sun from 11:00, Herengracht 605, tel. 020/523-1822, www.willetholthuysen.nl.*

Small Niche Museums

Museum of Bags and Purses (Tassenmuseum Hendrikje): This hardworking little museum fills an elegant 1664 canal house with 500 years of bag and purse history—from before the invention of pockets through the 20th century (€12.50, daily 10:00-17:00, behind Rembrandtplein at Herengracht 573, tel. 020/524-6452, www.tassenmuseum.nl).

Pipe Museum (Pijpenkabinet): This quirky-yet-classy museum holds 300 years of pipes in a 17th-century canal house. The (free)

street-level shop, Smokiana, sells new and antique pipes, various smoking curiosities, and scholarly books written by the shop's owner (€10, Mon-Sat 12:00-18:00, closed Sun, tel. 020/421-1779, just off Leidsestraat at Prinsengracht 488, www.pijpenkabinet.nl).

The Canal House (Het Grachtenhuis): Though promoted as a way to experience a great canalside mansion, this is basically a series of empty rooms showing videos—interesting but pricey (€12 in person, €10 online, Tue-Sun 10:00-17:00, closed Mon, Herengracht 386, www.hetgrachtenhuis.nl).

Southeast Amsterdam

Stretching from the edge of the Old City Center to the very outskirts, this neighborhood has a number of interesting sights, especially in the former Jewish Quarter. To reach the following sights from the train station, take tram #9 or #14. All of these sights (except the Tropical Museum) are close enough to be connected by tram, bike, or even on foot.

Waterlooplein and the Jewish Quarter

Several sights cluster near the large square, Waterlooplein, which grew up near the former Jewish Quarter. Survey the scene from the lamp-lined **Blauwbrug** ("Blue Bridge") over the Amstel River. From this point, the river is channeled to form the city's canals.

Scan clockwise. The big, curved, modern facade belongs to the **"Stopera,"** as it's the combo City Hall *(stadhuis)* and opera. Behind the Stopera (though not visible from the bridge) is the **Waterlooplein Flea Market.** Every day except Sunday, you'll find stalls selling cheap clothes, hippie stuff, old records, and tourist knickknacks.

To the right of the Stopera was the **former Jewish Quarter,** marked by the twin gray steeples of the Moses and Aaron Church. Since medieval times, Amsterdam had a thriving Jewish population. Jewish traders had long been welcome in a city that cared more about business than religion. By 1940, one in ten Amsterdammers was Jewish, and most lived in this neighborhood. But during the Nazi occupation, Jews were rounded up and shipped to extermination camps in Eastern Europe. By war's end, more than 100,000 of the country's 140,000 Jews had died. Today, about 25,000 Jews live in Amsterdam, and the Jewish Quarter has blended with the modern city.

Continue panning. That cute little **drawbridge,** while not famous,

is certainly photogenic. Beyond that is the city-block-sized **Hermitage Amsterdam.** Crossing the Amstel upstream is the **Magere Brug** ("Skinny Bridge")—one of the city's romantic spots.

▲Rembrandt's House (Museum Het Rembrandthuis)

A middle-aged Rembrandt lived here from 1639 to 1658 after his wife's death, as his popularity and wealth dwindled down to obscurity and bankruptcy. As you enter, ask when the next etching or painting demonstration is scheduled and pick up the excellent audioguide.

During your visit, you explore Rembrandt's reconstructed house, filled with exactly what his bankruptcy inventory of 1656 said he owned. Imagine him at work in his reconstructed studio. Marvel at his personal

Rembrandt's House has a modern entrance.

Gassan's free diamond-polishing demo

collection of exotic objects, many of which he included in paintings. At the etching demonstration, you learn about the etching process: drawing in soft wax on a metal plate that's then dipped in acid, inked up, and printed. For the finale, enjoy several rooms dedicated (generally) to original Rembrandt etchings. You're not likely to see a single Rembrandt painting, but this interesting museum may make you come away wanting to know more about the man and his art.

▸ *€12.50, includes audioguide, daily 10:00-18:00, etching and painting demonstrations almost hourly, Jodenbreestraat 4, tel. 020/520-0400, www.rembrandthuis.nl.*

▲Gassan Diamonds

Many shops in this "city of diamonds" offer tours. You get to see experts behind magnifying glasses polishing the facets of precious diamonds, followed by a visit to an intimate sales room to see (and perhaps buy) a mighty shiny yet very tiny souvenir.

▸ *Free, daily 9:00-17:00, a block from Rembrandt's House at Nieuwe Uilenburgerstraat 173-175, tel. 020/622-5333, www.gassan.com, handy WC.*

▲▲Hermitage Amsterdam

The famous Hermitage Museum in St. Petersburg, Russia loans part of its vast collection of art to Amsterdam. Amsterdam's Hermitage branch is the biggest of several in Europe, filling the Amstelhof, a 17th-century former nursing home that takes up a whole city block along the Amstel River.

The collection changes about every six months—check the museum's website to see what's on during your visit. Curators in Amsterdam

make a point to display art that complements—rather than just repeats—what the city's other museums show so well. The one small permanent History Hermitage exhibit explains the historic connection between the Dutch (Orange) and Russian (Romanov) royal families.

- *Generally €15, price varies with exhibit. Daily 10:00-17:00; come later in the day to avoid crowds. Mandatory free bag check, café. Located at Nieuwe Herengracht 14, tram #9 from the train station, recorded info tel. 020/530-7488, www.hermitage.nl.*

De Hortus Botanical Garden

A unique oasis of tranquility within the city, this large park is one of the oldest botanical gardens in the world, from 1638. As Dutch sailors roamed the globe, they returned with medicinal herbs, cacti, palm trees, and Europe's first coffee plant (brought from Ethiopia in 1706). Today, there are 6,000 different kinds of plants and several greenhouses (one for butterflies). No mobile phones are allowed, because "our collection of plants is a precious community—treat it with respect."

- *€8.50, not covered by Museumkaart, daily 10:00-17:00, Plantage Middenlaan 2A, tel. 020/625-9021, www.dehortus.nl, inviting Orangery Café serves tapas.*

▲Jewish Historical Museum (Joods Historisch Museum) and Portuguese Synagogue

A single ticket admits you to these two sights, located a half-block apart. The Jewish Historical Museum tells the story of the Netherlands' Jews through three centuries, serving as a good introduction to Judaism and Jewish traditions. The collection spreads across four historic former synagogues that have been joined by steel and glass to make one modern complex.

The centerpiece of the museum is the **Great Synagogue.** Take a seat and picture it during its prime (1671-1943): men worshipping downstairs, women above in the gallery. On the east wall (the symbolic direction of Jerusalem) were the Torah scrolls. The raised platform in the center of the room is where the text was sung.

Video displays around the room explain Jewish customs, from birth (circumcision) to puberty (the bar/bat mitzvah, celebrating the entry into adulthood) to Passover celebrations to marriage—culminating in the groom stomping on a glass while everyone shouts "Mazel tov!"

A Torah at the Jewish Historical Museum

Dutch Theater, where Nazis imprisoned Jews

Next, head upstairs where exhibits trace the history of Amsterdam's Jews from 1600 to 1900. From here, a sky bridge leads to the **New Synagogue** and the 20th century, including sobering artifacts from the devastating Nazi occupation.

Find contemporary exhibits in the **Aanbouw Annex,** then finish your visit by crossing the street to the **Portuguese Synagogue.** Built in the 1670s, it survived World War II, and stands today as a big, open, and simple place of worship.

▸ *€15, also covers Dutch Theater and National Holocaust Museum (see next listing), more for special exhibits; museum daily 11:00-17:00 (Portuguese Synagogue 10:00-16:00). Kosher café. Located at Jonas Daniel Meijerplein 2, tel. 020/531-0310, www.jhm.nl.*

▲Dutch Theater (Hollandsche Schouwburg), a.k.a. National Holocaust Memorial

Once a lively theater in the Jewish neighborhood, and today a moving memorial, this building was used as an assembly hall for local Jews destined for Nazi concentration camps. On the wall, 6,700 family names pay tribute to 107,000 Jews deported and killed by the Nazis. Some 70,000 victims spent time here, awaiting transfer.

Upstairs is a small-but-evocative history exhibit with a model of the ghetto, plus photos and memorabilia (such as shoes and letters) of some victims, putting a human face on the staggering numbers. Back in the ground-floor courtyard, notice the hopeful messages that visiting school groups attach to the wooden tulips.

▸ *Donation requested, free with Jewish Historical Museum/Portuguese*

Synagogue ticket, daily 11:00-17:00, Plantage Middenlaan 24, tel. 020/531-0380, www.hollandscheschouwburg.nl.

▲▲Dutch Resistance Museum (Verzetsmuseum)

Bam—it's May 1940 and the Germans invade the Netherlands, destroy Rotterdam, drive Queen Wilhelmina into exile, and—in four short days of fighting—hammer home the message that resistance is futile.

This museum tells the rest of the story—how the Dutch survived under Nazi occupation from 1940 to 1945. They faced a timeless moral dilemma: Is it better to collaborate with a wicked system to effect small-scale change—or to resist outright, even if your efforts are doomed to fail? You'll learn why some chose the former, and others the latter.

You'll see propaganda movie clips, study forged ID cards under a magnifying glass, and read about ingenious and courageous efforts—big and small—to undermine the Nazi regime. Vandals turned Nazi V-for-Victory posters into W-for-Wilhelmina. Printers circulated underground newspapers. Farmers organized a milk strike. Ordinary citizens hid radios under floorboards and Jews inside closets. They suffered through the "Hunger Winter" of 1944 to 1945, during which 20,000 died. Finally, it was springtime, the Allies liberated the country, and Nazi helmets were turned into Dutch bedpans.

▸ *€10, includes audioguide; Tue-Fri 10:00-17:00, Sat-Mon 11:00-17:00, mandatory and free bag check, Plantage Kerklaan 61, tel. 020/620-2535, www.verzetsmuseum.org.*

▲Tropical Museum (Tropenmuseum)

As close to the Third World as you'll get without lots of vaccinations, this imaginative museum offers wonderful re-creations of tropical life and explanations of Third World problems (largely created by Dutch colonialism and the slave trade). Ride the elevator to the top floor, and circle your way down through this immense collection, opened in 1926 to give the Dutch people a peek at their vast colonial holdings.

▸ *€15, daily 10:00-17:00, closed Mon off-season, tram #9 or #14 to Linnaeusstraat 2, cafeteria overlooks a park in back, tel. 020/568-8200, www.tropenmuseum.nl.*

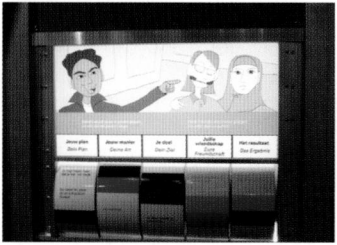

Dutch Resistance Museum makes you think.

NEMO's ship-shape science museum

Northeast Amsterdam

Central Library (Openbare Bibliotheek Amsterdam)

This huge, striking, multistory building holds almost 1,400 seats—many with wraparound views of the city—and lots of Internet terminals and Wi-Fi (€1/30 minutes). Everything's relaxed and inviting, from the fun kids' zone and international magazine and newspaper section on the ground floor to the rooftop cafeteria, with its dramatic view (€10 meals, salad bar).

▸ *Free, daily 10:00-22:00, a 10-minute walk east of Centraal station, tel. 020/523-0900, www.oba.nl.*

NEMO (National Center for Science and Technology)

This kid-friendly science museum is a city landmark. The distinctive copper-green structure (by well-known Italian architect Renzo Piano) juts up from the water like a sinking ship, prompting critics to nickname it the *Titanic*. The many exhibits, both permanent and temporary, allow you to explore science by playing with bubbles, giant dominoes, and room-size pinball machines. The museum's motto: "It's forbidden NOT to touch!" There's a rooftop restaurant with a great city view.

▸ *€15, June-Aug daily 10:00-17:30, Sept-May closed Mon, tel. 020/531-3233, www.e-nemo.nl. The roof terrace—open until 19:00 in the summer—is generally free. Located at Oosterdok 2, a 15-minute walk from Centraal station, or take bus #22 or #48 to the Kadijksplein stop.*

▲▲Netherlands Maritime Museum (Nederlands Scheepvaartmuseum)

Given the Dutch seafaring heritage, this is an appropriately big and impressive place.

The east building holds the core collection: globes, an exhibit on the city's busy shipping port, original navigational tools, displays of ship ornamentation, and paintings of dramatic 17th-century naval battles against the British. The west building has exhibits on whaling and of seafaring in the Dutch Golden Age.

Moored just outside is a replica of the *Amsterdam,* an 18th-century cargo ship of the Dutch East India Company (abbreviated VOC). Wander the decks, then duck your head and check out the captain and surgeon's quarters, and the hold. The ship is a little light on good historical information, but it's still shipshape enough to delight history buffs and *Pirates of the Caribbean* fans. The Royal Barge next door is no replica. Built for King William I in the early 19th century, this gaudy boat was purely ceremonial—a symbol of royal might.

▸ *€15, includes audioguide, daily 9:00-17:00, bus #22 or #48 from Centraal station to Kattenburgerplein 1, tel. 020/523-2222, www.scheepvaartmuseum.nl.*

▲EYE Film Institute Netherlands

This übersleek addition to the Amsterdam skyline is a film museum and cinema, located immediately across the water (the IJ) from Centraal station. The EYE (a play on "IJ") is a complex of museum spaces, theaters for art films, special exhibits, shops, and a trendy waterside terrace café. Helpful attendants at the reception desk can get you oriented. Check the website for the schedule of events.

▸ *General entry is free, films cost €10.50, and exhibits cost around €10 (credit cards only, no cash), exhibits 10:00-19:00, cinemas daily at 10:00 until last screening (ticket office usually closes at 22:00 or 23:00), tel. 020/589-1400, www.eyefilm.nl.*

Getting There: From the docks behind Centraal station, catch the free ferry (labeled Buiksloterweg) *across the river and walk left to the big white modern building.*

Day Trips

The Netherlands' efficient train system turns much of the country into a feasible day trip. Ask about "day return" tickets (same-day round trip) which are cheaper than two one-way tickets.

In Haarlem, the main church anchors a town that's both quaint and contemporary.

▲▲Haarlem

A half-hour away by train, the town of Haarlem is an agreeable mix of quaintness, history, and contemporary Dutch life.

The center of town is the massive main church, the **Grote Kerk.** Inside the church is Holland's largest organ (5,000 pipes) plus quirky exhibits like a replica of Foucault's pendulum and a 400-year-old cannonball. A spacious square **(Grote Markt)** surrounds the church. Sip a coffee or beer at one of the cafés, and take in a view that's looked much the same for 700 years and been captured in well-known paintings. The square hosts colorful market days on Monday (clothing) and Saturday (general).

Haarlem is the hometown of Frans Hals, and the **Frans Hals Museum** has the world's largest collection of his work. Stand eye-to-eye with life-size, lifelike, warts-and-all portraits of Golden Age brewers, preachers, workers, bureaucrats, and housewives. Most impressive are Hals' monumental group portraits.

The **Teylers Museum,** the Netherlands' oldest, almost feels like a

museum of a museum, with its well-preserved exhibits of fossils, minerals, and primitive electronic gadgetry.

The **Corrie ten Boom House** relates the inspirational story of a family that courageously hid Jews from the Nazis. Finally (two blocks northeast of Grote Markt, off Lange Begijnestraat), you can stroll through quaint Haarlem's cozy little **Red Light District.**

▸ *Trains to Haarlem depart Amsterdam's Centraal station every 30 minutes. From Haarlem's train station, the town center is a 10-minute walk—ask a local to point you to the "Grote Markt." There's a bike rental in the station. Avoid Haarlem on Mondays when many sights are closed. Haarlem's friendly TI (VVV) is in the Town Hall building on Grote Markt (tel. 023/531-7325, www.haarlem.nl).*

▲Other Dutch Destinations

The charming, canal-laced town of **Delft** (hometown of Vermeer and blue-painted ceramics) and its neighbor city, **The Hague** (famous for its Old Masters in the Maurithuis Gallery), make a rewarding day or two of sightseeing. **Arnhem** has the Arnhem Open-Air Folk Museum and the Kröller-Müller Museum of Van Gogh paintings (in Hogue Veluwe National Park). The **Historic Triangle** offers a nostalgic loop trip on a steam train and boat. **Keukenhof's** flower garden is one of the world's best (open in spring only). College-town **Leiden** is the Netherlands' answer to Cambridge or Oxford, while mighty **Rotterdam**—bombed during World War II—is now Europe's largest port with a gleaming skyline. Medieval **Utrecht** is known for its lively downtown core and Holland's top railway museum.

If you want more, there's also **Edam** (an adorable village), **Alkmaar** (best on Friday for its cheese market), **Aalsmeer** (a bustling modern flower auction), **Schokland** (for a chance to walk on what was the bottom of the sea at this village/museum), and open-air folk museums at **Enkhuizen** and **Zaanse Schans.**

For more info on these places visit www.holland.com.

Sleeping

I've grouped my hotel listings into four neighborhoods: **West Amsterdam** (quiet canals, charming gabled buildings), **Central Amsterdam** (shopping and tourist sights, though a bit gritty), the **Southern Canal Belt** (restaurants and nightlife while still cozy), and **Southwest Amsterdam** (a semi-suburban neighborhood around Vondelpark and Museumplein).

I like hotels that are clean, central, reasonably priced, friendly, small enough to have a hands-on owner and stable staff, and run with a respect for Dutch traditions.

Book as far in advance as possible, as Amsterdam is busy from mid-March to October.

A Typical Amsterdam Hotel Room

Amsterdam is a tough city for budget accommodations. A typical double room in Amsterdam will be small by American standards. It will have one double bed (either queen-sized or slightly narrower) or two twins. There's probably a bathroom in the room with a toilet, sink, and bathtub or shower. The room has a telephone and TV, and may have a safe. Almost all accommodations have free Wi-Fi. Single rooms, triples, and quads will have similar features.

Breakfast—sometimes included in the room price—is normally a self-service buffet of fresh bread, cereal, ham, cheese, yogurt, juice, and coffee or tea.

Canal houses were built tight. They have steep stairs with narrow treads; almost none have elevators. If steep stairs are potentially problematic, book a hotel with an elevator.

Making Reservations

Reserve your rooms several weeks or even months in advance—or as soon as you've pinned down your travel dates. Especially busy are late March to May (tulips in bloom), summer weekends, September (conventions), and some national holidays (e.g., King's Day in late April). Make reservations by phone, through the hotel's website, or with an email that covers:

- the size of your party and type of rooms you need
- your arrival and departure dates, written European-style—day followed by month and year (for example, 18/06/18 or 18 June 2018); include the total number of nights
- special requests (such as en suite bathroom vs. down the hall, cheapest room, twin beds vs. double bed, quiet room)
- applicable discounts (such as a Rick Steves reader discount, cash discount, or promotional rate)

If they require your credit-card number for a deposit, you can send it by email (I do), but it's safer via phone, the hotel's secure website, or split between two emails. Once your room is booked, print out the confirmation, and reconfirm your reservation with a phone call or email a day or two in advance (alert them if you'll be arriving after 17:00). If canceling a reservation, some hotels require advance notice—otherwise they may bill you. Even if there's no penalty, it's polite to give at least three days' notice.

Hotel Price Code

$$$$	**Splurge:** Most rooms over €170
$$$	**Pricier:** €130-170
$$	**Moderate:** €90-130
$	**Budget:** €50-90
¢	**Backpacker:** Under €50
RS%	**Rick Steves discount**

These rates are for a standard double room with breakfast in high season. For the best prices, book directly; if the listing includes RS%, request a Rick Steves discount.

Budget Tips

To get the best rates, book directly with the hotel, not through a third-party site. Start with the hotel's website, looking for promo deals. Check rates every few days, as prices can vary greatly based on demand. Email several hotels to ask for their best price and compare offers—you may be astonished at the range. Some may give a discount if you stay at least three nights or pay in cash.

Besides hotels, there are cheaper alternatives. Bed-and-breakfasts (B&Bs) offer a personal touch at a fair price—I've listed several. I also list a few all-ages hostels, which offer €25-30 dorm beds (and a few inexpensive doubles) and come with curfews and other rules.

Renting an apartment can save money if you're traveling as a family, staying more than a week, and planning to cook your own meals. I list two local services—Truelove and Frederic—or try www.airbnb.com, www.homeaway.com, or www.vrbo.com.

Don't be too cheap when picking a place to stay. Anything under €130 (even my listings) can be a little rough around the edges. Choose a nice, central neighborhood. Construction noise is common in always-renovating Amsterdam, so consider asking for a quiet room in back. Your Amsterdam experience will be more memorable with a welcoming oasis to call home.

WEST AMSTERDAM: Tree-lined canals, gabled buildings, and candlelit restaurants; just minutes on foot to Dam Square. Many of my hotels are old mansions—charming but with lots of steep stairs.	
$$$$ The Toren Keizersgracht 164 tel. 020/622-6033, www.thetoren.nl	Renovated chandeliered mansion by peaceful canal, classy yet friendly, elevator, breakfast extra, RS%
$$$$ Hotel Ambassade Herengracht 341 tel. 020/555-0222, www.ambassade-hotel.nl	Elegant and fresh, palatial public areas, top-notch staff, air-con, elevator, breakfast extra, RS%
$$$ Hotel Brouwer Singel 83 tel. 020/624-6358, www.hotelbrouwer.nl	Woody and old-timey, tranquil yet central, canal views, elevator, reserve way ahead, cash only
$$$ The Times Hotel Herengracht 135 tel. 020/330-6030, www.thetimeshotel.com	Business-comfort hotel in scenic canal setting, modern rooms are tight but have bathtubs, elevator, breakfast extra
$$$ Wiechmann Hotel Prinsengracht 328 tel. 020/626-3321, www.hotelwiechmann.nl	Spacious, sparsely furnished dark-wood rooms, cozy public areas, Old World charm, canal views
$$$ Hotel Hegra Herengracht 269 tel. 020/623-7877, www.hotelhegra.nl	Nine cozy rooms in old canalside townhouse, great location, breakfast extra
$$$ Mr. Jordaan Hotel Bloemgracht 102 tel. 020/626-5801, www.mrjordaan.nl	34 newly renovated rooms, funky-but-stylish touches, budget rooms very tight, breakfast extra, elevator
$$$ Max Brown Hotel Herengracht 13 tel. 020/522-2345, www.maxbrownhotels.com	Boutique chain hotel with trendy urban design, hipster clientele, mod rooms and public areas, canal views
$$$ Maes B&B Herenstraat 26, tel. 020/427-5165, www.bedandbreakfastamsterdam.com	Great value, tastefully cozy and antique-filled, use of kitchen, warm hosts
$$$ Herengracht 21 B&B Herengracht 21 tel. 020/625-6305, mobile 06-2812-0962, www.herengracht21.nl	Two stylish, intimate rooms in art-filled canal house, lovely host

$$ Hotel Hoksbergen Singel 301 tel. 020/626-6043, www.hotelhoksbergen.com	Budget option for canalside location, expect cramped rooms and a lived-in feel, steep stairs
$$ Hotel Van Onna Bloemgracht 104 tel. 020/626-5801, www.hotelvanonna.nl	Simple industrial-strength rooms, leafy canal views, cozy attic rooms
$$ Frederic Rent-a-Bike & Guestrooms Brouwersgracht 78 tel. 020/624-5509, www.frederic.nl	Various private rooms on gorgeous canal, from dumpy to elegant (see website), no breakfast
$$ Truelove Guesthouse Prinsenstraat 4 mobile 06-5334-0866, info@truelovegesthouse.com	Room-rental service rents homey furnished apartments with kitchens
¢ The Shelter Jordan Bloemstraat 179 tel. 020/624-4717, www.shelter.nl	90-bed hostel, bunk beds in dorms, friendly, Christian-run, near Anne Frank House
CENTRAL AMSTERDAM: Ideal for shopping, tourist sights, and public transportation, but the area has traffic noise and urban grittiness, and the hotels can lack character.	
$$$ Hotel Résidence Le Coin Nieuwe Doelenstraat 5 tel. 020/524-6800, www.lecoin.nl	42 larger-than-average rooms with kitchenettes, breakfast extra, near Mint Tower
$$$ Hotel Ibis Amsterdam Centre Stationsplein 49 tel. 020/721-9172, www.ibishotel.com	Huge modern place by Centraal station, full comfort but no charm, breakfast extra, book long in advance
$$$ Hotel Nes Kloveniersburgwal 137 tel. 020-624-4773, www.hotelnes.com	Boutique hotel with 36 tight but modish rooms, some canal views, often books up six months in advance, breakfast extra, elevator
¢ The Shelter City Barndesteeg 21 tel. 020/625-3230, www.shelter.nl	Hostel in Red Light District, well-run and safe, evening Bible study

SOUTHERN CANAL BELT: Mom-and-pop B&B-style coziness within a five-minute walk of restaurants and rowdy nightlife. Walk or easy tram to the center of town or Museumplein.	
$$$ Hotel de Leydsche Hof Leidsegracht 14 tel. 020/638-2327, mobile 06-3099-2744, www.freewebs.com/leydschehof	B&B, hidden gem, large white rooms, views of canal or leafy yard, lots of stairs, friendly owners, cash only
$$$ Wildervanck B&B Keizersgracht 498 tel. 020/623-3846, www.wildervanck.com	Family-run, two tasteful rooms in an elegant old canal house, pleasant breakfast room, cash only
SOUTHWEST AMSTERDAM: Semi-suburban neighborhood within walking distance of Vondelpark and Museumplein. Good-value modern accommodations (elevators) but less Old World charm. Trams #1, #2, #5 to/from Centraal station.	
$$$ Hotel Piet Hein Vossiusstraat 51 tel. 020/662-7205, www.hotelpiethein.nl	81 stylishly sleek rooms, some air-con, swanky lounge, pleasant garden, quiet street, breakfast extra
$$$ Hotel Fita Jan Luijkenstraat 37 tel. 020/679-0976, www.fita.nl	20 bright rooms, 100 yards from Van Gogh Museum, modern yet rustic, many amenities, free laundry service, warm welcome
$$ Hotel Alexander Vondelstraat 44 tel. 020/589-4020, www.hotelalexander.nl	34 modern rooms on quiet street, some overlook garden patio, breakfast extra
$$ Bed & Breakfast Amsterdam Sloterkade 65 tel. 020/679-2753, www.bedandbreakfastamsterdam.net	Cozy and bright rooms, some on a canal, friendly husband-wife owners, no elevator, cash only
$ Hotel Parkzicht Roemer Visscherstraat 33 tel. 020/618-1954, www.parkzicht.nl	13 big, plain, old-fashioned rooms, steep stairs, some street noise, cheaper rooms with shared bath
¢ Stayokay Vondelpark (IYHF) Zandpad 5 tel. 020/589-8996, www.stayokay.com	Hostel in Vondelpark, lots of beds, family rooms, reserve well ahead, over-25s feel welcome

Eating

Amsterdam's thousand-plus eateries make for a buffet of dining options. Choose from elegant candlelit restaurants, an exotic Indonesian *rijsttafel,* a light meal outdoors alongside a canal, a herring snack at a fish stand, or stopping by a takeout stand for "Flemish" fries with mayonnaise. Besides meals, the Dutch spend endless hours sitting and drinking at outdoor cafés. Budget some money—and time—to sightseeing for your palate.

My listings are in Amsterdam's atmospheric neighborhoods, handy to recommended hotels and sights. Most are in West Amsterdam (near the Anne Frank House and the Jordaan—the most charming place to dine), Central Amsterdam (around Dam Square, Spui, and the Mint Tower), and Southwest Amsterdam (close to museums and recommended hotels).

No matter where you dine, expect it to be *gezellig*—a much-prized Dutch virtue, meaning an atmosphere of relaxed coziness.

Restaurant Price Code

$$$$	**Splurge:** Most main courses over €20
$$$	**Pricier:** €15-20
$$	**Moderate:** €10-15
$	**Budget:** Under €10

Based on the average cost of a typical main course. A *friets* stand or other takeout spot is **$**; a basic café or sit-down eatery is **$$**; a casual but more upscale restaurant is **$$$**; and a swanky splurge is **$$$$**.

When in Amsterdam...

When in Amsterdam, I eat on the Dutch schedule. For breakfast, I eat at the hotel (bread, meat, cheese, egg) or grab a pastry and coffee at a café. Lunch (12:00-14:00) is a simple sandwich *(broodje)* or soup. In between meals, I might stop at a takeout stand for french fries *(friets)* or a pickled herring. In the late afternoon, Amsterdammers enjoy a beverage with friends at an outdoor table on a lively square. Dinner (18:00-21:00) is the biggest meal of the day, the time for slowing down and savoring a multi-course restaurant meal.

Restaurants

As English is spoken everywhere, and the Dutch take an elegant-but-casual approach to dining, there's no need to learn a lot of special Dutch etiquette. At Dutch restaurants that have waitstaff, 15 percent service is included in the menu price, although it's common to round up the bill after a good meal (usually 5-10 percent). The Dutch are willing to pay for bottled water with their meal (Spa brand is popular, sparkling or still), but free tap water is always available upon request. All Dutch eateries are now non-smoking.

Cafés and Bars

Besides full-service restaurants, there are other places to fill the tank. An *eetcafé* is a simple restaurant serving meat-and-potatoes fare in a

no-nonsense setting. A *salon de thé* serves tea and coffee, but also pastries and sandwiches.

Cafés are all-purpose establishments, serving light meals at mealtimes and coffee, drinks, and snacks the rest of the day. At night, cafes are essentially "bars," catering to the drinking crowd. *Bruin* cafés ("brown cafés") have a more traditional wood-paneled ambience. A "coffeeshop" is the code word for a café where marijuana is sold and consumed, though most offer drinks and munchies, too.

Cafés and bars with outdoor tables generally do not charge more if you sit outside (unlike in France or Italy). When ordering drinks in a café or bar, you can just pay as you go (especially if the bar is crowded), or wait until the end to settle up, as many locals do. If you get table service, take the cue from your waiter. There's no need to tip if you order at the counter, but if you get table service, it's nice to round up to the next euro ("keep the change").

Most cafés have a light-fare menu of sandwiches, salads, and soups, but some offer more ambitious meals. Throughout the day they cater to customers who just want to relax over a drink.

The Dutch love their coffee, enjoying many of the same drinks (espresso, cappuccino) served in American or Italian coffee shops. A *koffie verkeerd* (fer-KEERT, "coffee wrong") is an espresso with a lot of steamed milk. Many cafés/bars have a juicer for making fresh-squeezed orange juice, and they'll have the full array of soft drinks.

Order "a beer," and you'll get a *pils*—a light pilsner-type beer in a 10-ounce glass with a thick head leveled off with a stick. Typical brands are Heineken, Grolsch, Oranjeboom, Amstel, and the misnamed Bavaria (brewed in Holland). Belgian beers are also popular.

The Dutch enjoy a chilled shot of *jenever* (yah-NAY-ver), a Dutch gin made from juniper berries. *Jong* (young) is sharper; *oude* (old) is mellow and more expensive. You'll find a variety of local fruit brandies and cognacs. The Dutch people drink a lot of fine wine, but it's almost all imported.

A quarter of Dutch people smoke tobacco. Holland has a long tradition as a smoking culture, being among the first to import the tobacco plant from the New World. Healthy, tanned, sixty-something Dutch people sip their beer, take a drag, and ask me why Americans murder themselves with Big Macs. Nevertheless, Dutch law has outlawed smoking tobacco almost everywhere indoors: restaurants, cafés and bars...and even marijuana-dealing coffeeshops.

Picnicking

Amsterdam makes it easy to turn a picnic into a first-class affair. Grab something to go and enjoy a bench in a lively square or with canalside ambience.

Sandwiches *(broodjes)* of delicious cheese or ham on fresh bread are cheap at snack bars and delis. You'll find takeout stands selling herring, french fries, and ethnic foods.

Albert Heijn grocery stores (daily 8:00-22:00) have great deli sections with picnic-perfect takeaway salads and sandwiches. There are handy locations near the Westerkerk, Dam Square, the Mint Tower, and inside Centraal station (find them on the map on page 153).

Traditional Dutch Cuisine

Traditional Dutch cooking is basic and hearty—meat or fish, soup, fresh bread, boiled potatoes, cooked vegetables, and salad. Mashed potato dishes (*stamppot* or *hutspot*) served with meat and vegetables is classic Dutch comfort food. But these days, many Dutch people have traveled and become more sophisticated, enjoying dishes from around the world.

The Dutch are better known for their informal foods. Pickled herring *(haring)* come with onions or pickles on a bun. French fries *(Vlaamse friets)* are eaten with mayonnaise rather than ketchup. Popular Dutch cheeses are Edam (covered with red wax) or Gouda (HOW-dah). *Kroketten* (croquettes) are log-shaped rolls of meats and vegetables (kind of like corn dogs) breaded and deep-fried. *Pannenkoeken* (pancakes) can be either sweet dessert pancakes or crêpe-like, savory pancakes eaten as a meal.

For dessert, try *pannenkoeken, poffertjes* (small, sugared puffy pancakes), *stroopwafels* (syrup waffles), and *appelgebak* or *appeltaart* (apple pie).

Ethnic

Since its Golden Age days as a global trader, Amsterdam has adopted food from other lands.

Indonesian *(Indisch),* from this former Dutch colony, is commonly served as a *rijsttafel* (literally, "rice table"), a multidish sampler of many spicy dishes and rice or noodles. A *rijsttafel* can be split between two hungry tourists. Various other menu items *(nasi rames, bami goring, nasi goring)* are also multidish meals. Common Indonesian sauces are peanut, red chili *(sambal),* and dark soy.

You'll find Middle Eastern *shoarma* (roasted lamb in pita bread), falafel, gyros, or a *döner kebab.*

Surinamese *(Surinaamse),* from the former colony on the northeast coast of South America, is a mix of Caribbean and Indonesian influences. The signature dish is *roti* (spiced chicken wrapped in a tortilla) and rice (white or fried) served with meats in sauces (curry and spices).

Alstublieft: Wherever you eat in Amsterdam—at fine restaurants, dim cafes, or the pickled herring shack—you'll constantly hear servers saying *"Alstublieft"* (AHL-stoo-bleeft). It's a useful, catchall polite word, meaning "please," "here's your order," "enjoy," and "you're welcome." You can respond by saying, *"Dank u wel"* (dahnk yoo vehl)—thank you.

CENTRAL AMSTERDAM: Eateries along the spine of the old center, from Centraal station to Dam Square to the Mint Tower (see map pages 152-153)		
1	**$$$ Restaurant Kantjil en de Tijger** Spuistraat 291 tel. 020/620-0994	Indonesian, thriving and noisy, good-value *rijsttafel,* reservations smart (daily 12:00-23:00)
2	**$ Kantjil To Go** Nieuwezijds Voorburgwal 342 tel. 020/620-3074	Indonesian takeout bar, split a large box on Spui Square for delicious cheap meal (daily 12:00-21:00)
3	**$$ Café 't Gasthuys** Grimburgwal 7 tel. 020/624-8230	Brown café on canal, busy dumbwaiter cranks out light lunches and OK dinners (daily 12:00-16:30 & 17:30-22:00)
4	**$$-$$$ De Jaren Café** Nieuwe Doelenstraat 20 tel. 020/625-5771	Modern, chic, and inviting; upstairs restaurant (w/salad bar), downstairs café (light lunch or drink), view deck (daily 9:30-24:00)
5	**$$ Pannenkoekenhuis Upstairs** Grimburgwal 2 tel. 020/626-5603	For pancakes, tiny characteristic perch up steep stairs (Tue-Fri 12:00-19:00, closed Mon)
6	**$$ La Place Cafeteria** Kalverstraat 203 tel. 020/622-0171	Fresh and appealing cafeteria at the end of Kalverstraat near the Mint Tower (Sun-Mon 11:00-19:00, Tue-Wed 10:00-19:30, Thu-Sat 10:00-21:00)
7	**$ Atrium University Cafeteria** Oudezijds Achterburgwal 237 tel. 020/525-3999	Ultra-cheap student cafeteria serves anyone (Mon-Fri 11:00-15:00 & 17:00-19:30, closed Sat-Sun)
8	**$$ Van Kerkwijk** Nes 41 tel. 020/620-3316	Popular, unpretentious, quirky eatery with loyal following, no written menu, fresh international dishes (daily 11:00-23:00)
9	**$ De Zeevang Haring** corner of Nieuwezijds Voorburgwal and Raadhuisstraat tel. 020/423-4283	Dutch herring stand just behind the Royal Palace at a busy intersection (closed Sun-Mon)
10	**$ Stubbe's Haring** At locks on Singel canal	Traditional takeout herring sandwiches from well-established place (Tue-Sat 10:00-18:00, closed Sun-Mon)

11	**Albert Heijn Supermarkets** Nieuwezijds Voorburgwal 226; Koningsplein 4; Westermarkt 21 and Centraal station	Grocery stores with good deli sections handy for picnics, no US credit cards (daily 8:00-22:00)
WEST AMSTERDAM: Charming canals near the Anne Frank House and Jordaan residential neighborhood (see map pages 152-153)		
12	**$$$$ Max Restaurant** Herenstraat 14 tel. 020/420-0222	Upscale Indonesian with French influences, choose from a short list to assemble two- or three-course meal, outdoor seating, no-frills interior, reservations recommended (dinner Tue-Sun 18:00-22:00, closed Mon)
13	**$$ De Bolhoed** Prinsengracht 60 tel. 020/626-1803	Serious vegetarian and vegan, colorful setting, big splittable portions (daily 12:00-22:00)
14	**$$$ Café Restaurant de Reiger** Nieuwe Leliestraat 34 tel. 020/624-7426	Bistro ambience, classic Jordaan scene, fresh fish and French-Dutch cuisine, crowded late (daily 17:00-24:00)
15	**$$ Café 't Smalle** Egelantiersgracht 12 tel. 020/623-9617	Simple light lunches, Belgian beer, good wine, canalside deck (daily 11:00-late)
16	**$$ Kinnaree Thai Restaurant** Eerste Anjeliersdwarsstraat 14	Freshly prepared Thai cuisine with modern ambience, attentive waitstaff (daily 17:30-22:00)
17	**$$$ Ristorante Hostaria** Tweede Egelantiersdwarsstraat 9 tel. 020/626-0028	Tight, steamy Italian place with fun energy and open kitchen (Tue-Sun 18:00-22:00, closed Mon)
18	**$$ Winkel** Noordermarkt 43 tel. 020/623-0223	Easygoing cornerside hangout, Euro-Dutch meals outside or in, great *appeltaart* (Mon-Sat 8:00-late, Sun from 10:00)
19	**$$ The Pancake Bakery** Prinsengracht 191 tel. 020/625-1333	Fun and creative menu with lots of hearty savory and dessert pancakes, popular with backpackers (daily 9:00-21:30, American breakfasts until noon)

20	**$$ Café van Zuylen** Torensteeg 4 tel. 020/639-1055	Big, upscale café with outdoor seating right by bridge; glassed-in front room, classy back room; salads, burgers, local fare, Dutch and Belgian beers (open long hours daily)
21	**$$$ Ristorante Toscanini** Lindengracht 75 tel. 020/623-2813	Upmarket Italian, lively and always packed, reservations essentially required (Mon-Sat 18:00-22:30, closed Sun)
22	**$$ Café Villa Zeezicht** Torensteeg 7 tel. 020/626-7433	Classic European café at Torensluis Bridge, so-so menu but great *appeltaart* and people-watching (daily 9:00-21:30)
23	**$ Café 't Papeneiland** Prinsengracht at #2 tel. 020/624-1989	For drinks only (except for famous apple pie), classic old brown café with canal views, local scene may feel cold to tourists (daily 10:00-24:00)
SOUTHWEST AMSTERDAM: Near Museumplein, Vondelpark, and Leidseplein (see map pages 152-153)		
24	**$-$$$ "Restaurant Row"** Lange Leidsedwarsstraat	Various eateries of every price and cuisine, on street near Leidseplein
25	**$$ Café Gruter** Willemsparkweg 73 tel. 020/679-6252	Neighborhood hangout just outside Vondelpark with classic brown café interior, seating on square (lunch daily 11:00-16:00, also serves dinner, open very late)
26	**$$ Café Loetje** Johannes Vermeerstraat 52 tel. 020/662-8173	Pub grub and beer with a rollicking neighborhood-beer-hall feel, three dining zones (daily 11:00-late)

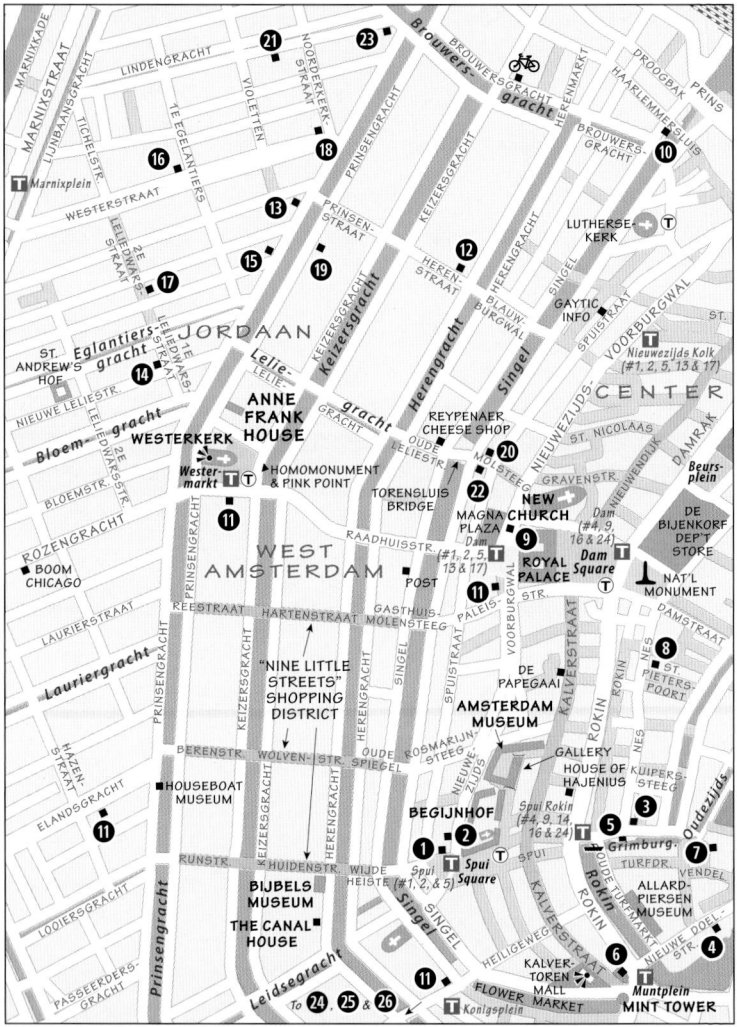
MARNIXKADE
MARNIXSTRAAT
LINDENGRACHT
LUNBAANSGRACHT
TICHELSTR.
VIOLETTEN
NOORDERKERKSTRAAT
TE EGELANTIERS
PRINSENGRACHT
Brouwers-gracht
BROUWERSGRACHT
HEREENMARKT
DROOGBAK
PRINS
HAARLEMMERSLUIS
BROUWERS-GRACHT
Marnixplein
WESTERSTRAAT
PRINSEN-STRAAT
KEIZERSGRACHT
LUTHERSE-KERK
LEIEDWARS-STRAAT
HEREN-STRAAT
HERENGRACHT
BLAUW-BURGWAL
SINGEL
GAYTIC INFO
SPUISTRAAT
VOORBURGWAL
ST.
Nieuwezijds Kolk (#1, 2, 5, 13 & 17)
Eglantiers gracht
JORDAAN
ST. ANDREW'S HOF
Lelie-gracht
LELIE
Keizersgracht
Herengracht
Singel
NIEUWEZIJDS-CENTER
NIEUWE LELIESTR.
LEIEDWARSSTR.
Bloem-gracht
WESTERKERK
ANNE FRANK HOUSE
REYPENAER CHEESE SHOP
OUDE LELIESTR.
MOLSTEEG
ST. NICOLAAS
DAMRAK
Beurs-plein
Wester-markt
HOMOMONUMENT & PINK POINT
TORENSLUIS BRIDGE
GRAVENSTR.
NIEUWENDIJK
NEW CHURCH
MAGNA PLAZA
Dam (#4, 9, 16 & 24)
DE BIJENKORF DEP'T STORE
BLOEMSTR.
ROZENGRACHT
BOOM CHICAGO
WEST AMSTERDAM
RAADHUISSTR.
Dam (#1, 2, 5, 13 & 17)
ROYAL PALACE
Dam Square
NAT'L MONUMENT
POST
PALEIS-STR.
DAMSTRAAT
LAURIERSTRAAT
REESTRAAT
HARTENSTRAAT
GASTHUIS-MOLENSTEEG
VOORBURGWAL
KALVERSTRAAT
ST. PIETERS-POORT
Lauriergracht
"NINE LITTLE STREETS" SHOPPING DISTRICT
DE PAPEGAAI
AMSTERDAM MUSEUM
ROKIN
NES
BERENSTR.
WOLVEN-STR.
OUDE SPIEGEL
ROSMARIJN-STEEG
GALLERY
HOUSE OF HAJENIUS
KUIPERS-STEEG
HAZEN-STRAAT
ELANDSGRACHT
HOUSEBOAT MUSEUM
BEGIJNHOF
Spui Rokin (#4, 9, 14, 16 & 24)
Grimburg
Oudezijds
RUNSTR.
HUIDENSTR.
WIJDE HEISTR.
Spui
Spui Square
SPUI
TURFDR.
VENDEL
BIJBELS MUSEUM
THE CANAL HOUSE
LOOIERSGRACHT
Prinsengracht
Leidsegracht
HEILIGEWEG
KALVERSTRAAT
ALLARD-PIERSEN-MUSEUM
NIEUWE DOELEN STR.
KALVER-TOREN MALL
Muntplein
MINT TOWER
FLOWER MARKET
Koningsplein
PASSEERDERS-GRACHT
To 24, 25 & 26

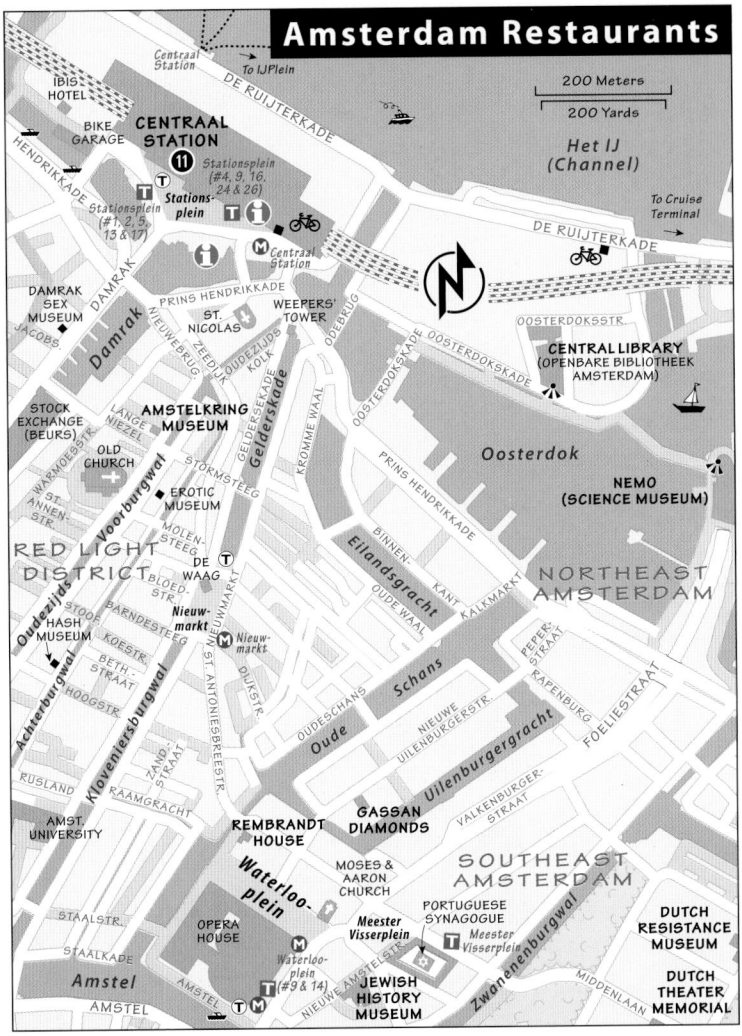
Amsterdam Restaurants
Centraal Station
To IJPlein
DE RUIJTERKADE
200 Meters
200 Yards
IBIS HOTEL
BIKE GARAGE
CENTRAAL STATION
Stationsplein (#4, 9, 16, 24 & 26)
Stations-plein
Stationsplein (#1, 2, 5, 13 & 17)
HENDRIKKADE
Centraal Station
Het IJ (Channel)
To Cruise Terminal
DE RUIJTERKADE
DAMRAK SEX MUSEUM
DAMRAK
PRINS HENDRIKKADE
ST. NICOLAS
WEEPERS' TOWER
JACOBS
Damrak
NIEUWEBRUG
ZEEDIJK
OUDEZIJDS KOLK
ODEBRUG
OOSTERDOKSSTR.
OOSTERDOKSKADE
CENTRAL LIBRARY (OPENBARE BIBLIOTHEEK AMSTERDAM)
STOCK EXCHANGE (BEURS)
LANGE NIEZEL
AMSTELKRING MUSEUM
OLD CHURCH
WARMOESTR.
ST. ANNEN-STR.
Voorburgwal
STORMSTEEG
GELDERSKADE
Geldersk ade
KROMME WAAL
EROTIC MUSEUM
MOLEN-STEEG
Oosterdok
NEMO (SCIENCE MUSEUM)
PRINS HENDRIKKADE
BINNEN-
RED LIGHT DISTRICT
DE WAAG
BLOED-STR.
Eilandsgracht
KANT
KALKMARKT
NORTHEAST AMSTERDAM
OUDE WAAL
Oudezijds
HASH MUSEUM
STOOF
BARNDESTEEG
Nieuw-markt
Nieuw-markt
NIEUWMARKT
PEPER-STRAAT
KOESTR.
BETH.-STRAAT
HOOGSTR.
ST. ANTONIESBREESTR.
DUKSTR.
Schans
RAPENBURG
FOELIESTRAAT
Achterburgwal
Kloveniersburgwal
OUDESCHANS
Oude
NIEUWE UILENBURGERSTR.
Uilenburgergracht
ZAND-STRAAT
RUSLAND
RAAMGRACHT
VALKENBURGER-STRAAT
AMST. UNIVERSITY
REMBRANDT HOUSE
GASSAN DIAMONDS
SOUTHEAST AMSTERDAM
Waterloo-plein
MOSES & AARON CHURCH
PORTUGUESE SYNAGOGUE
Meester Visserplein
Meester Visserplein
STAALSTR.
OPERA HOUSE
STAALKADE
Waterloo-plein (#9 & 14)
DUTCH RESISTANCE MUSEUM
Amstel
AMSTEL
NIEUWE AMSTELSTR.
JEWISH HISTORY MUSEUM
Zwanenenburgwal
MIDDENLAAN
DUTCH THEATER MEMORIAL
AMSTEL

Practicalities

Planning 156
Money 157
Arrival in Amsterdam 158
Helpful Hints 160
Getting Around Amsterdam 161
Staying Connected 165
Sightseeing Tips 167
Theft and Emergencies 168
Activities 169
Dutch Phrases 177

PLANNING

Amsterdam's best travel months—also the busiest and most expensive for flights and hotels—are late March through September. In spring, the weather is cool, but the nearby tulip fields are flowering, drawing surprisingly big crowds that drive up Amsterdam hotel prices. Summer brings the best weather (it's rarely too hot) and equally big crowds. In September, Amsterdam hosts seasonal conferences (again, drawing crowds). Amsterdam in winter is cold and rainy, but the crowds are fewer, cafés are cozy, and the city feels lively but not touristy.

Make sure your passport is up to date (to renew, see www.travel.state.gov). Call your debit- and credit-card companies about your plans. Book hotel rooms well in advance, especially for peak season (late March-Sept) and three-day holiday weekends (find a list at www.iamsterdam.com). Consider buying travel insurance. To avoid long lines, consider getting advance tickets (especially in peak season) for the Rijksmuseum and Van Gogh Museum. Smart travelers reserve their Anne Frank House tickets exactly two months in advance. If you're traveling beyond Amsterdam, research rail passes, train reservations, and car rentals.

Helpful Websites

Amsterdam Tourist Information: www.iamsterdam.com
The Netherlands' Tourist Information: www.holland.com
Passports and Red Tape: www.travel.state.gov
Cheap Flights: www.kayak.com (for international flights), www.skyscanner.com (for flights within Europe)
Airplane Carry-on Restrictions: www.tsa.gov
European Train Schedules: www.bahn.com
General Travel Tips: www.ricksteves.com (helpful info on train travel, rail passes, car rental, travel insurance, packing lists, and much more—plus updates to this book)

MONEY

The Netherlands uses the euro currency: 1 euro (€1) = about $1.10. To convert euros to dollars add about 10 percent: €20 = about $22, €50 = about $55. (Check www.oanda.com for the latest exchange rates.)

Withdraw money from an ATM (known as a *geldautomaat* in the Netherlands) using a debit card, just like at home. Visa and MasterCard are commonly used throughout Europe. Before departing, call your bank or credit-card company: Ask about international transaction fees and alert them that you'll be making withdrawals in Europe, and if you don't know it, get your credit card PIN. Many travelers bring a second debit/credit card as a backup. Many Amsterdam merchants prefer cash, and some places—even major grocery stores—won't accept foreign credit cards at all, so withdraw large amounts (€250-300) from the ATM.

While American credit cards are accepted almost everywhere in Europe, even newer chip-style cards may not work in some payment machines (e.g., ticket kiosks). If your card is rejected, be prepared to pay with cash, find a nearby cashier who can swipe it, or try entering your PIN.

To keep your cash and valuables safe, wear a money belt. But if you do lose your credit or debit card, report the loss immediately with a collect phone call: Visa (tel. 303/967-1096), MasterCard (tel. 636/722-7111), and American Express (tel. 336/393-1111).

ARRIVAL IN AMSTERDAM

Amsterdam's Schiphol Airport

Schiphol (SKIP-pol) is very user-friendly. Though it officially has four terminals, it's really just one big building. You could walk it end to end in about 20 minutes. All terminals have ATMs, banks, shops, bars, and free Wi-Fi. For airport information, call toll tel. 0900-0141 (from other countries dial +31-20-794-0800), or visit www.schiphol.nl (airport code: AMS).

Baggage-claim areas for all terminals empty into the same arrival zone, officially called Schiphol Plaza but generally signed simply *Arrivals Hall*. Here you'll find a busy TI (near Terminal 2, daily 7:00-22:00), a train station, and bus stops for getting into the city. Service Point (near Terminal 4) sells SIM cards, prints train tickets, and ships packages. The "Train Tickets and Services" counter (near Burger King) provides all sorts of train ticket and info services without the long lines of Amsterdam's Centraal station. The train ticket machines in the hall accept US credit cards if they have a chip and you know the PIN.

To get between Schiphol and downtown Amsterdam (10 miles away), you have several options:

Train: Direct trains to Amsterdam's Centraal station run frequently from Schiphol Plaza (4-6/hour, 20 minutes, €5.20). Schiphol's train station also serves other destinations including Delft, The Hague, Rotterdam, Bruges, and Brussels.

Shuttle Bus: The Connexxion shuttle bus departs from lane A7 in front of the airport and takes you directly to most hotels. There are three different routes, including one to the Westerkerk (near some of my recommended hotels). Ask the attendant which one works best for you (2/hour, 20-45 minutes from first to last hotel, €17 one-way, €27 round-trip). For trips from Amsterdam to Schiphol, reserve at least two hours ahead (tel. 088-339-4741, www.airporthotelshuttle.nl).

Public Bus: Bus #197 (departing from lane B9 in front of the airport) is handy for those going to the Leidseplein district (€5, buy ticket from driver). If you're staying in the city of Haarlem, catch #300 from lane B4.

Taxi or Uber: Allow about €50 to downtown Amsterdam by regular taxi. Uber serves the airport for about €28.

Amsterdam's Centraal Train Station

Amsterdam Centraal is truly central. You're within walking distance of Dam

Square, and all the transportation options (tram, bus, taxi, Metro, and rental bikes) are right out front.

The station is fully equipped for the traveler. A Service Point store in the northern section sells SIM cards, mails packages, and prints tickets (daily 7:00-22:00). Luggage lockers are in the east corridor, under the "B" end of the platforms (always open, can fill up on busy summer weekends). The station has two handy Albert Heijn supermarkets and plenty of eateries (especially near platform 2; try the venerable First Class Grand Café). Ticket machines accept chip-and-PIN cards only; if you don't have a chip, the staff in the ticket office can process the transaction.

Exiting the station, you're in the heart of the city. Straight ahead is Damrak street, leading to Dam Square (a 10-minute walk). To your left are the main TI, the GVB public-transit office, and the MacBike bike rental (in the station building, see page 162). To the right of the station are the postcard-perfect neighborhoods of West Amsterdam; some of my recommended hotels are within walking distance.

The city's blue trams are easy to use—just buy a ticket or pass from the conductor. Trams #1, #2, and #5 (which run to nearly all my recommended hotels) leave from in front of the station's main entrance. All trams leaving Centraal station stop at Dam Square along their route. For more on the transit system, see page 163.

Arrival by Cruise Ship: The Passenger Terminal Amsterdam (PTA) is a mile east of Centraal station, an easy 15-minute walk along the water. Or catch tram #26 (buy ticket from conductor). A taxi to, say, the Rijksmuseum, would cost about €16.

HELPFUL HINTS

Tourist Information (TI): The Dutch name for a TI is "VVV," pronounced "fay fay fay." Amsterdam's main TI—across the street from Centraal station—is crowded and sometimes inefficient, and the free maps are poor quality. The TIs sell good city maps (€2.50) and the *A-Mag* entertainment guide (€3.50). A second official Centraal station TI (labeled "I Amsterdam Store") is in the new section on the north side and is much less crowded (Mon-Sat 8:00-19:00 except Thu-Sat until 20:00, Sun 9:00-18:00).

English Bookstores: For fiction and guidebooks, try the **American Book Center** (at Spui 12, Mon 12:00-20:00, Tue-Sat 10:00-20:00, Sun 11:00-18:30, tel. 020/535-2575) or the huge and helpful **Scheltema** (at Rokin 9, daily 10:00-19:00, tel. 020/523-1411).

Maps: The *Carto Studio Centrumkaart Amsterdam* is top-notch (€2.50). Online, check out the "Go Where the Locals Go" city map at www.amsterdamanything.nl.

Hurdling the Language Barrier: This is one of the easiest places in the non-English-speaking world for an English speaker. Nearly all signs and services are offered in both Dutch and English. Pronunciation, however, can be tough: Dam (pronounced dahm), Damrak (DAHM-rock), Spui (spow, rhymes with cow), Rokin (roh-KEEN), Kalverstraat (KAL-ver-straht), Leidseplein (LIDE-zuh-pline), Jordaan (yor-DAHN), and *gracht* (a canal, pronounced hrockt). To learn a few Dutch pleasantries, see page 177.

Time: The Netherlands' time zone is six/nine hours ahead of the east/west coasts of the US.

Business Hours: Most businesses are open roughly 9:00-19:00 on weekdays, Saturday from 9:00 until midafternoon, and closed Sundays. The first Sunday of the month, many stores open for "shopping Sunday" *(koopzondag)*. Boutique-type shops have slightly different hours: Tuesday to Saturday 10:00-18:00, Sunday-Monday 12:00-18:00 (and some stay open until 21:00 on Thursday).

Watt's Up? Europe's electrical system is 220 volts, instead of North America's 110 volts. You'll need an adapter plug with two round prongs, sold inexpensively at travel stores in the US. Most newer electronics (such as laptops, hair dryers, and battery chargers) convert automatically, so you won't need a separate converter.

Tipping

Tipping in the Netherlands isn't as generous as it is in the US. To tip a taxi driver, round up to the next euro (for a €4.50 fare, give €5). For longer rides, figure about 5-10 percent. At hotels, if you let the porter carry your luggage, tip a euro for each bag. For sit-down service in a restaurant, a 15 percent service charge is always already included in the list price of the food, although it's common to round up the bill after a good meal (usually 5-10 percent).

Numbers and Stumblers: What Americans call the second floor of a building is the first floor in Europe. Europeans write dates as day/month/year. Commas are decimal points and vice versa—a dollar and half is 1,50, and there are 5.280 feet in a mile. The Netherlands uses the metric system: A kilogram is 2.2 pounds; a liter is about a quart; and a kilometer is six-tenths of a mile. Temperature is measured in Celsius: 0°C = 32°F. To roughly convert Celsius to Fahrenheit, double the number and add 30.

Laundry: In the Jordaan, try Clean Brothers Wasserij (Westerstraat 26, €7 self-service, €9 ready in an hour, tel. 020/627-9888). Near Leidseplein, try Powders (Kerkstraat 56, self-service or drop-off, mobile 06-5741-2403). Or ask your hotelier for the nearest location.

Pedestrian Safety: Beware of silent transportation—trams, electric mopeds, and bicycles—when walking around town. Don't walk on tram tracks or pink/maroon bicycle paths. Before you step off any sidewalk, do a double- or triple-check in both directions to make sure all's clear.

Best Views: Although sea-level Amsterdam is notoriously horizontal, there are a few high points where you can get the big picture. The best city views are from the Central Library (see page 133), the Westerkerk tower (see page 93), the Old Church (Oude Kerk, see page 74), and the rooftop terrace at the NEMO science museum (see page 133).

GETTING AROUND AMSTERDAM

I get around Amsterdam by walking, biking, and taking the occasional tram. The longest walk a tourist would make is an hour from Centraal

station to the Rijksmuseum. Pedestrians should be extremely vigilant for silent but potentially painful bikes, trams, and crotch-high bollards.

By Bike

Everyone—bank managers, students, pizza delivery boys, and police—uses this mode of transport. It's by far the smartest way to travel in a city where 40 percent of all traffic rolls on two wheels. Consider renting a bike for a few days, chain it to the rack outside your hotel at night, and enjoy wonderful mobility.

One-speed bikes, with *"brrringing"* bells, rent for about €10/day (must leave ID, deposit, or credit-card imprint). Your hotel can direct you to the nearest rental shop. Star Bikes Rental, a five-minute walk east of Centraal station, is cheap (€7/day, €17/3 days, De Ruyterkade 143, tel. 020/620-3215, www.starbikesrental.com). MacBike, at the east end of Centraal station, is the biggest (€9.75/24 hours, €6/extra day, tel. 020/624-8391, www.macbike.nl).

No one here wears a helmet. They do, however, ride cautiously, and so should you: Use arm signals, follow the bike-only traffic signals, stay in the obvious and omnipresent bike lanes, yield to traffic on the right, dismount and walk your bike through pedestrian zones. Fear oncoming trams. Carefully cross tram tracks at a perpendicular angle to avoid catching your tire in the rut. Bike theft is rampant—follow your rental agency's locking directions (usually involving two locks) to the letter. A handy bicycle route-planner can be found at www.routecraft.com (select "bikeplanner," then click British flag for English). For a "Do-It-Yourself Bike Tour of Amsterdam" and for bike tours, see "Activities," later in this chapter.

By Tram, Bus, and Metro

Amsterdam's public transit system includes trams, buses, and an underground Metro. Of these, trams are most useful for most tourists.

Tickets and Day Passes: A single ticket costs €2.90 and is good for one hour on the tram, bus, and Metro, including transfers. You can board any tram or bus and buy a ticket from the conductor with no extra fee. Given how expensive single tickets are, consider getting a pass: I find a pass to be the simplest option when staying in Amsterdam for a few days. A 24-hour pass is €7.50 (€12.50/48 hours, €17/72 hours, €21.50/96 hours). Tickets and passes are sold on board, at Metro-station vending machines (cash or European credit card only), at GVB public-transit offices, at TIs, and at some souvenir shops. Note that the I Amsterdam sightseeing card (page 168) includes a transit pass.

If you're staying longer than three or four days and plan to use Dutch trains as well as trams and buses, your best option is the **TripKey pass,** which offers discounted rates on buses, trams, and trains. The pass costs €3.50 and is linked to your credit-card account, so fares are charged as you go (you never need to reload). You can buy a TripKey pass when you get to the Netherlands, but it's more convenient to order it online before your trip and pick it up at a handy location such as Schiphol Airport (at the Hertz car rental desk), Amsterdam Centraal station (at the DoubleTree by Hilton hotel), or at many other hotels, car rental desks, and TIs. For more information or to order a pass, visit www.tripkey.nl or call 088-934-3443.

Riding Trams: Board at any door that's not marked with a red/white "do not enter" sticker. If you need a ticket or pass, pay the conductor (in a booth at the back); if there's no conductor, pay the driver in front. You must always "check in" as you board by scanning your ticket or pass at the pink-and-gray scanner, and "check out" by scanning it again when you get off. The scanner will beep and flash a green light after a successful scan. Don't accidentally scan twice while boarding, or it becomes invalid.

Trams #2 *(Nieuw Sloten)* and #5 *(A'veen Binnenhof)* travel the north-south axis, from Centraal station to Dam Square to Leidseplein to Museumplein (Van Gogh and Rijks museums). Tram #1 (marked *Osdorp*) also runs to Leidseplein. At Centraal station, these three trams depart from the west side of Stationsplein (with the station behind you, they're to your right).

Tram #14, which doesn't connect to Centraal station, goes east-west (Westerkerk-Dam Square-Muntplein-Waterlooplein-Plantage). If you get

lost in Amsterdam, don't sweat it—10 of the city's 17 trams take you back to Centraal station.

Buses and Metro: Though few tourists use the bus and Metro, they work the same as the trams—scan your ticket or pass as you enter and again when you leave. The Metro system is scant—used mostly for commuting to the suburbs—but it does connect Centraal station with some sights east of Damrak (Nieuwmarkt-Waterlooplein-Weesperplein).

Other Transport

Taxi and Uber: Amsterdam is not a good town for taxis, thanks to circuitous streets and pricey fares. The drop charge is a steep €7 for the first two kilometers (e.g., from Centraal station to the Mint Tower), after which it's €2.12 per kilometer. Wave taxis down, find a rare taxi stand, or call 020/677-7777. Uber works in Amsterdam like in the US; even your US app will work, but you'll need to use Wi-Fi or get a data plan that covers you while traveling.

Bike Taxis: These hard-working entrepreneurs (found particularly near Dam Square and Leidseplein) wheel you wherever you want. But negotiate the price before you board (no meter). Typical fares are €1/3 minutes, no surcharge for baggage (Leidseplein to Anne Frank House is about €6).

Tourist Canal Boats: Though most canal boats are meant for round-trip sightseeing cruises, a few companies make stops along the way that can work well for point-to-point travel. Check the brochures or websites for Rederij P. Kooij (tel. 020/623-3810, www.rederijkooij.nl), Blue Boat Company (tel. 020/679-1370, www.blueboat.nl), or Gray Line (tel. 020/217-0500, www.canal.nl). For basic tourist sightseeing rides, see "Activities," later in this chapter.

By Car: If you've got a car, park it—all you'll find are frustrating

one-way streets, terrible parking, and meter maids with a passion for booting cars. Park in a central garage (€70/day), or at a park-and-ride lot on the outskirts (follow *P&R* signs from freeway, €8/24 hours) and take transit into the city center. Ask your hotel for parking advice.

STAYING CONNECTED

You can bring your own mobile device (phone, tablet, laptop) and follow my budget tips. Or buy a European SIM card for your phone. Or just use European landlines (in your hotel room) and computers (there's usually one in your hotel lobby). These options are described in full at www.ricksteves.com/phoning.

Making Calls

To **call the Netherlands from a US or Canadian phone:** Dial 011 (international access code), 31 (the Netherlands' country code), and the phone number.

To **call the Netherlands from a European phone:** Dial 00, then 31 followed by the phone number.

To **make calls within the Netherlands:** If you're dialing from a Dutch mobile phone or landline within the same city, just dial the phone

Useful Phone Numbers

Police, Ambulance, or Fire: 112

US Consulate: Amsterdam, tel. 020/575-5309, after-hours emergency tel. 070/310-2209, Museumplein 19, must make appointment at http://amsterdam.usconsulate.gov

US Embassy: The Hague, tel. 070/310-2209, visits by appointment only, Lange Voorhout 102, http://netherlands.usembassy.gov

Canadian Embassy: The Hague, tel. 070/311-1600, consular services Mon-Fri 9:30-12:30, closed Sat-Sun, Sophialaan 7, www.canada.nl

Collect Calls to the US: Tel. 0800-022-9111

number, with no area code. If calling outside your area code, dial both the area code (starts with 0) and the local number.

To **call from the Netherlands to another country:** Dial 00, the country code (for example, 1 for the US or Canada), and then the number.

Initial Zero: Drop the initial zero from international phone numbers (except when calling Italy).

Mobile Tip: Pressing the + sign auto-selects the correct international access code.

Budget Tips for Using Your Mobile Device in Europe

Use free Wi-Fi whenever possible. Unless you have an unlimited data plan, save most of your online tasks for Wi-Fi. Many hotels and cafés have Wi-Fi for guests.

Sign up for an international plan. Most providers offer a global plan that cuts the cost of calls and texts, and gives you a block of data. Your normal plan may already include international coverage.

Minimize the use of your cellular network. If you can't find Wi-Fi, you can roam on your cellular network. When you're done, avoid further charges by disabling cellular data or roaming in your settings. Save bandwidth-gobbling tasks (Skyping, downloading apps, streaming) for when you're on Wi-Fi.

Use calling/messaging apps for cheaper calls and texts. Some apps (Skype, Viber, FaceTime, Google+ Hangouts) let you call or text for free or cheap when you're on Wi-Fi.

Buy a European SIM card: This option helps you get faster data connections and make voice calls at cheap local rates. Buy a basic phone in Europe (about $40 from a phone shop) or bring an "unlocked" US phone from home. Once you insert a European SIM, you'll have a European phone number. Buy a new card when you arrive in a new country (sold at phone shops, newsstands, vending machines, and department-store electronics counters).

Stick to landlines: If it's inexpensive to make calls from your hotel-room phone (ask at the desk for rates before you dial), you can make your calls even cheaper by using an international phone card (sold at many newsstands, street kiosks, tobacco shops, and train stations).

SIGHTSEEING TIPS

Hours: Hours of sights can change unexpectedly, so confirm the latest times from a TI, at the sight's website, or at the general website **www.iamsterdam.com.** Many sights stop admitting people 30-60 minutes before closing time, and guards start shooing people out before the actual closing time, so don't save the best for last.

What to Expect: Important sights such as the Rijksmuseum have metal detectors or conduct bag searches that will slow your entry. Many of Amsterdam's sights require you to check even small daypacks and coats—usually for free, often in coin-op lockers where you get your coin back.

Photos and videos are normally allowed, but flashes or tripods usually are not. Many sights offer guided tours and rent audioguides (€4-7). Expect changes—artwork can be in restoration or on tour. Most have an on-site café.

Discounts: Many sights offer free or reduced admission for children under 18 and for students (with International Student Identity Cards, www.isic.org). Senior discounts are generally only for EU residents, but it's worth asking.

Free Rick Steves Audio Tours: I've produced free audio tours covering some of Amsterdam's best sights, including the Amsterdam City Walk, the Jordaan Walk, and the Red Light District Walk. You can download Rick Steves Audio Europe via Apple's App Store, Google Play, or the Amazon Appstore.

Advance Tickets and Sightseeing Passes

You can avoid long ticket lines (common from late March-Oct) at the Rijksmuseum, Van Gogh Museum, and Anne Frank House by booking tickets in advance or getting a sightseeing pass. (But note that nobody can skip security lines.) If you're visiting off-season, these strategies are less important, especially if you use my other crowd-beating tips.

Advance Tickets: It's smart to buy tickets online through each museum's website, generally with no extra booking fee. Just print out your ticket and bring it to the ticket-holder's line for a quick entry. You can also buy advance tickets at TIs (though lines there can be long). Another line-skipping option is a sightseeing pass. Read on...

Museumkaart (€60): This sightseeing pass—which covers many

museums throughout the Netherlands for 31 days—can save money and time. For example, if you visit the Rijksmuseum, Van Gogh Museum, Anne Frank House, and Amsterdam Museum, the pass almost pays for itself. Plus, it lets you skip the ticket lines (except at the Anne Frank House). Check www.amsterdam.info for a list of which sights are included, and do the math. The Museumkaart is sold at all participating museums—buy it at a less-crowded one to avoid lines.

Other Sightseeing Passes: Though not as good a deal for most people, the **I Amsterdam card** covers many Amsterdam sights (including a canal boat ride) and includes a transportation pass. But it does not cover the Rijksmuseum, Anne Frank House, or museums outside of Amsterdam, and it lets you skip lines only at the Van Gogh Museum. Get details at www.iamsterdamcard.com.

THEFT AND EMERGENCIES

Theft: While violent crime is rare in the city center, thieves (mainly pickpockets) thrive near famous monuments, on public transportation, at places of drunkenness, in hostels, or anywhere crowds press together. Be alert to the possibility of theft, even when you're absorbed in the wonder and newness of Amsterdam. Smartphones are thief-magnets. So are rental bikes (see page 162). I keep my valuables—passport, credit cards, crucial documents, and large amounts of cash—in a money belt that I tuck under my beltline. Dial 112 for English-speaking police help. To replace a passport, file the police report, then call your consulate or embassy to make an appointment (US consulate, tel. 020/575-5309, http://amsterdam.usconsulate.gov).

Medical Help: Dial 112 for a medical emergency. Most doctors speak English. For minor ailments, do as the Dutch do and first visit a pharmacy, where qualified technicians routinely diagnose and prescribe. There's a one-stop-shopping pharmacy near Leidseplein named "DA" Dienstdoende Apotheek (Leidsestraat 74-76, daily until 22:00, tel. 020/627-5351) and another near Dam Square, called BENU Apotheek (Damstraat 2, daily until 17:00, tel. 020/624-4331). Otherwise, ask your hotelier for assistance.

ACTIVITIES

Shopping

Amsterdam brings out the browser even in those who were not born to shop. Modish boutiques, open-air markets, quirky souvenirs, and pleasant neighborhoods can make window-shopping a ▲▲▲ sightseeing experience.

Most shops are open Tuesday-Saturday 10:00-18:00, Sunday-Monday 12:00-18:00, and some stay open until 21:00 on Thursdays. The TIs have a free *Shopping in Amsterdam* brochure.

Department Stores: For essential items, try all-purpose Hema (Mon-Sat 9:00-19:00, Thu until 21:00, Sun 11:00-18:30, at Centraal station and Kalverstraat 212). The De Bijenkorf department store on Dam Square is old-time fancy, with a little view café on the first floor. The Magna Plaza (a block west of Dam Square) is a stylish mall of 40 boutiques.

Shopping Neighborhoods: The central axis of streets from Centraal station to Leidseplein—essentially, the route of the Amsterdam City Walk—is the busiest shopping corridor in town. It includes Kalverstraat (pedestrian-only but soulless) and Leidsestraat (with trendy, elegant shops).

In West Amsterdam, the **Jordaan,** with its main drag Westerstraat, is a veritable wonderland of funky, artsy shops (especially on Monday, when a street market appears nearby). **The Nine Little Streets** (De Negen Straatjes) is a tic-tac-toe of streets that's home to diverse shops and trendy cafés. The center is approximately where Wolvenstraat crosses the Keizersgracht and Herengracht canals (just west of the Amsterdam Museum).

The Southwest Amsterdam (Museumplein) neighborhood has two of the city's ritziest zones. **Spiegelkwartier** (stretching north from the

Rijksmuseum along Spiegelgracht and Nieuwe Spiegelstraat) is *the* place for art and antiques. **P. C. Hooftstraat** is the city's most expensive shopping street, located between Museumplein and Vondelpark.

Open-Air Markets: These are museums for people-watchers. Ten general markets, open six days a week (generally 9:30-17:00, closed Sun), keep folks who brake for garage sales pulling U-turns. Try the flower market near the Mint Tower (see page 31). The Waterlooplein Flea Market (daily except Sun near Waterlooplein Metro station) has stalls of garage-sale junk/treasure. The huge Albert Cuyp street market is Amsterdam's biggest, bustling daily 9:00-17:00. You'll find fish, exotic vegetables, bolts of fabric, pantyhose, bargain clothes, native Dutch and ethnic food stands (especially *stroopwafels* and Surinamese *rotis*), and great people-watching. It's located a 10-minute walk east of Museumplein and a block south of the Heineken Experience (tram #16 or #24).

Souvenirs: You won't need a guidebook to find plenty of shops selling wooden shoes, blue-and-white delftware (ranging from inexpensive fireplace titles to very expensive antiques), *jenever* (Dutch gin made from juniper berries, sold in traditional stone bottles), chocolate (Verkade or Droste cocoa in tins), or flower seeds and bulbs (be sure they're US Customs-friendly).

Art-themed items (Rembrandt posters, Van Gogh coffee mugs) are popular—try the Van Gogh Museum bookshop. Amsterdam's rare bookstores have old books and maps. Marijuana pipes must be absolutely clean and unused to get through US Customs (and even then they may hassle you on legal technicalities). To mail your purchases home, ask your hotelier for the nearest ersatz post office, or use Service Point, a shipping service at Schiphol Airport and Centraal station.

Getting a VAT Refund: If you purchase more than €50 worth of goods at a single store, you may be eligible to get a refund of the 21 percent Value-Added Tax (VAT). Have the store fill out the paperwork, then get it stamped at the airport by Customs and processed by a VAT refund company (e.g., Global Blue or Premier Tax/Travelex, located in Schiphol's departure halls). Get more details from your merchant or see www.ricksteves.com/vat.

Customs for American Shoppers: You are allowed to take home $800 worth of items per person duty-free, once every 31 days. You can also bring back one liter of alcohol duty-free. As for food, you can take home many processed and packaged foods (e.g., vacuum-packed cheeses, chocolate, mustard) but no fresh produce or meats. Any liquid-containing

foods must be packed in checked luggage, a potential recipe for disaster. To check customs rules and duty rates, visit www.help.cbp.gov.

Nightlife

Many Amsterdam hotels serve breakfast until 11:00 because so many people—visitors and locals—live for nighttime in this city.

On summer evenings, people flock to the main squares for drinks at outdoor tables. **Leidseplein** is the liveliest square, surrounded by theaters, restaurants, and nightclubs. The slightly quieter **Rembrandtplein** (with adjoining Thorbeckeplein and nearby Reguliersdwarsstraat) is the center of gay clubs and nightlife. **Spui** features a full city block of bars. The **Red Light District** (particularly Oudezijds Achterburgwal) is less sleazy, even festive, in the early evening (before 22:00).

For a list of current events, look for the *A-Mag* entertainment guide or Dutch newspapers (Thu editions generally list events). *Uitkrant* magazine is in Dutch, but anyone can figure out an event and its date, time, and location (available at TIs, bars, and bookstores).

Classical Music: The Concertgebouw is the main venue, located at the far south end of Museumplein (free 12:30 lunch concerts on Wed, tel. 0900-671-8345, www.concertgebouw.nl). For chamber music and contemporary works, visit the Muziekgebouw aan 't IJ, near the train station (Piet Heinkade 1, tel. 020/788-2000, www.muziekgebouw.nl). For opera and dance, try the Stopera at Amstel 3 (tel. 020/625-5455, www.operabal let.nl). In the summer, Vondelpark hosts open-air concerts.

The Westerkerk has free lunchtime concerts most Fridays at 13:00 (May-Oct only, Prinsengracht 281, tel. 020/624-7766, www.westerkerk.nl). The New Church on Dam Square offers periodic organ concerts (tel. 020/638-6909, www.nieuwekerk.nl). The Red Light District's Old

Church (Oude Kerk) has carillon concerts Tuesday and Saturday at 16:00 (Oudekerksplein, tel. 020/625-8284, www.oudekerk.nl).

Rock, Jazz, Hip-Hop: Two clubs near Leidseplein present big-name acts that you might recognize...if you're younger than I am: Melkweg (Lijnbaansgracht 234a, tel. 020/531-8181, www.melkweg.nl) and Paradiso (Weteringschans 6, tel. 020/626-4521, www.paradiso.nl). Jazz has a long tradition at the Bimhuis nightclub, now located at the Muziekgebouw by Centraal station (Piet Heinkade 3, great views from the bar, tel. 020/788-2188, www.bimhuis.com).

Boom Chicago: This R-rated comedy improv act (in English) has been entertaining tourists and locals for years, with raucous skits about Dutch culture and local tourism. It erupts nightly at the theater at Rozengracht 117 (€22-27, ticket office open daily from 15:00, no shows Mon, tel. 020/217-0400, www.boomchicago.nl).

Theater: Amsterdam is one of the world centers for experimental live theater (much of it in English). Many theaters cluster around the street called the Nes, which stretches south from Dam Square.

Movies: Many theaters run movies in their original language. It's

not unusual for showings to be sold out—consider buying tickets during the day. Two memorable places to see a movie are the classic Tuschinski Theater (see page 126) and the splashy EYE Film Institute (page 134).

Late-Night Museums: The Anne Frank House is open daily until 22:00 from April through October, and Saturday until 21:00 in the off-season. The Stedelijk Museum stays open until 22:00 on Friday from March through October, and the Van Gogh Museum is open until 22:00 on Friday year-round. Amsterdam's marijuana and sex museums are always open until at least 22:00.

Marijuana (a.k.a. Cannabis)

Smoking marijuana—which was decriminalized in the Netherlands decades ago—causes about as much excitement here as a bottle of beer. You can buy it in licensed "coffeeshops" and smoke it there. In many places, the prospective customer has to initiate the transaction by asking the bartender to show them the cannabis menu or display case. You can buy either hashish (the dried sap of the cannabis plant) or the leaf of the plant (which the Dutch call "marihuana" or "grass"). Shops generally sell prerolled joints (€4-5) and baggies (€8-15). Prerolled joints are either blended with tobacco or "pure," meaning the pot is blended with a nontobacco herb mix. Any place that caters to Americans will have joints without tobacco, but you have to ask specifically for a "pure" joint.

Most shops have loaner bongs or rolling papers. You can smoke your marijuana in any coffeeshop (regardless of where you bought it), so long as you buy a drink or snack. There are always new proposals afloat to try to ban marijuana—stay tuned.

Of Amsterdam's many coffeeshops, here are a few that have a mellow atmosphere that's welcoming to first-time Americans: Paradox is the most *gezellig* (cozy), a graceful place that also serves light meals (two blocks west of Anne Frank House at Eerste Bloemdwarsstraat 2, tel. 020/623-5639, www.paradoxcoffeeshop.com). The Grey Area is two blocks east of the Anne Frank House (Oude Leliestraat 2, tel. 020/420-4301, www.greyarea.nl). The Bulldog Café is the big franchise brand, with one right on Leidseplein (Leidseplein 17, tel. 020/625-6278, www.thebulldog.com).

Canal Boat Tours

These long, low, tourist-laden boats offer a relaxing one-hour introduction to the city (with uninspiring recorded headphone commentary). Several

different companies offer similar services: Boats depart every 15-30 minutes from various docks around town. Some operate only by day (generally 10:00-18:00), but some have night cruises, when bridges are illuminated. Choose your boat company based on convenience of its starting point. Tip: Boats leave only when full, so jump on a full boat to avoid waiting at the dock.

Rederij P. Kooij is cheapest; boats dock opposite Centraal station (€9, boats until 22:00 in summer, tel. 020/623-3810, www.rederijkooij.nl). Blue Boat Company is near Leidseplein (€16 or €14 online, runs daily 10:00-18:00; €19.50 or €17.50 online for night cruises until 22:00 by reservation, Stadhouderskade 30, tel. 020/679-1370, www.blueboat.nl). Gray Line is opposite Centraal station (€16, nightly until 22:00; Prins Hendrikkade 33a, tel. 020/217-0500, www.canal.nl).

Paddleboats: For do-it-yourself canal tours and lots of exercise, rent these "canal bikes" from Canal Bus, near the Anne Frank House, Rijksmuseum, and Leidseplein (€8/hour per person, daily July-Aug 10:00-21:00, Sept-June 10:00-18:00).

Guided Tours

For an entertaining three-hour group tour that gives a once-over of central Amsterdam, try the enthusiastic-but-amateur New Europe "Free" Tours (truly free but tips expected, leave from Dam Square, www.neweuropetours.eu).

If you'd like a private guide to anywhere in Amsterdam, Albert Walet is knowledgeable (€70/2 hours for up to 4 people, mobile 06-2069-7882, abwalet@yahoo.com). In the Red Light District, Randy Roy's Red Light Tours offers group tours nightly at 20:00 that are fun and informative (€15, mobile 06-4185-3288, www.randyroysredlighttours.com).

Do-It-Yourself Bike Tour of Amsterdam

For a good day trip enjoying the bridges, bike lanes, and sleepy, off-the-beaten-path canals, try this route:

Start at Centraal station. Head west down Haarlemmerstraat, working your wide-eyed way down Prinsengracht (drop into Café 't Papeneiland at Prinsengracht 2) and detouring through the small, gentrified streets of the Jordaan neighborhood before popping out at the Westerkerk under the tallest spire in the city.

Pedal south to the lush and peaceful Vondelpark, then cut back through the center of town: Leidseplein, the Mint Tower, and along Rokin street to Dam Square. From there, cruise the Red Light District, following Oudezijds Voorburgwal past the Old Church (Oude Kerk) to Zeedijk street, and return to the train station.

Then, you can escape into the countryside by hopping on the free ferry (free for both you and your bike) to the north bank of the North Sea Canal. Behind Centraal station are docks with four ferries, leaving every few minutes. The middle two ferries shuttle immediately across the harbor (a 3-minute ride). From there, you can ride your bike two kilometers (1.25 miles) along the canal, through suburbs, and into the *polderland* and villages. Amsterdam is gone, and you're rolling through your very own Dutch painting.

Guided Bike Tours: Yellow Bike Guided Tours takes groups of people on a variety of two- to three-hour routes, either in-city or to the countryside (€22.50-32.50, bike rental included, leave from Nieuwezijds Kolk 29 near Centraal station (reservations smart, tel. 020/620-6940, www.yellowbike.nl). Joy Ride Bike Tours offers private 4.5-hour tours as well as custom theme tours, starting near the Rijksmuseum (€33, mobile 06-4361-1798, www.joyridetours.nl).

RESOURCES FROM RICK STEVES

This Pocket guide is one of dozens of titles in my series of guidebooks on European travel. I also produce a public television series, *Rick Steves' Europe,* and a public radio show, *Travel with Rick Steves.* My website, www.ricksteves.com, offers a wealth of free travel information, including videos and podcasts of my shows and classes, audio tours of Europe's great sights, travel forums, guidebook updates, my travel blog, and my guide to European rail passes—plus an online travel store and information on our tours of Europe.

How Was Your Trip? You can share your tips, concerns, and discoveries at www.ricksteves.com/feedback. I value your feedback. Thanks in advance.

Dutch Phrases

You won't need to learn Dutch, but at least learn a few pleasantries to connect with the locals.

The all-purpose word *alstublieft* (AHL-stoo-bleeft) can mean "please," "thanks," or "You're welcome."

Hello.	**Hallo.**	hol-LOH
Good day.	**Dag.**	dahhh
Good morning.	**Goeiemorgen.**	hhhoy-ah MOR-hhhen
Yes	**Ja**	yah
No	**Nee**	nay
Please	**Alstublieft**	AHL-stoo-bleeft
Thank you.	**Dank u wel.**	dahnk yoo vehl
Excuse me.	**Pardon.**	par-DOHN
Do you speak English?	**Spreekt u Engels?**	spraykt oo ENG-els
Goodbye.	**Tot ziens.**	toht zeens
one / two / three	**een / twee / drie**	ayn / t'vay / dree
What does it cost?	**Wat kost?**	vaht kost
I would like...	**Ik wil graag...**	ik vil hhhrahhhk
...a room.	**...een kamer.**	un kah-mer
...a ticket.	**...een kaart.**	un kart
...a bike.	**...een fiets.**	un feets
Where is...?	**Waar is...?**	vahr is
...the station	**...het station**	het sta-tsee-on
...the tourist info office	**...de VVV**	duh fay fay fay
left / right	**links / rechts**	links / rechts
open / closed	**open / gesloten**	"open" / hhhe-sloh-ten
menu	**menu**	muh-NOO
with / without	**met / buiten**	met / bow-ten
and / or	**en / of**	en / of
bread	**brood**	broht
salad	**sla**	slah
cheese	**kaas**	kahs
water	**water**	WAH-tuhr
beer	**bier**	beer
wine	**wijn**	wayn
coffee	**koffie**	"coffee"
tea	**thee**	tay
I am vegetarian.	**Ik ben vegetarish.**	ik ben vay-hhhe-tah-rish
Tasty.	**Lekker.**	lek-ker
Enjoy!	**Smakelijk!**	smak-kuh-luk
Cheers!	**Proost!**	prohst
The bill, please.	**De rekening, alstublieft.**	duh RAY-kun-ing AHL-stoo-bleeft

INDEX

A

Aalsmeer: 136
Aanbouw Annex: 131
Accommodations: *See* Sleeping
Airport, Schiphol: 158
Air travel, websites: 156
Albert Cuyp street market: 170
Albert Heijn Supermarkets: 147, 150
Alkmaar: 136
Almond Blossom (Van Gogh): 67–68
Alstublieft: 148
American Book Center: 160
American Express: 157
Amstelkring Museum: 8, 77–78, 118–119
Amstel River: 15, 18, 23, 127
Amsterdam (cargo ship): 134
Amsterdam Museum: 8, 25–27, 118
Anne Frank House: 95, 101–112, 120; late-night hours, 11, 173; maps, 103, 108; orientation, 8, 102; self-guided tour, 103–112
Arnhem: 136
Arrival in Amsterdam: 158–159
Art museums: daily reminder, 11; Amsterdam Museum, 8, 25–27; Frans Hals Museum (Haarlem), 135; Hermitage Amsterdam, 8, 129–130; Museum Het Rembrandthuis, 9, 128–129; Stedelijk Museum, 8, 123; Teylers Museum (Haarlem), 135–136; Willet-Holthuysen Museum, 9, 126. *See also* Rijksmuseum; Van Gogh Museum
ATMs: 157
Audio Tours, Rick Steves: 167

B

Bags and Purses, Museum of: 126
Banana Bar: 81–82
Bars: 144–146, 171
Bedroom, The (Van Gogh): 62
Beer: 146; Heineken Experience, 124
Begijnhof: 9, 27–28, 116
Beurs van Berlage: 19
Bike taxis: 164
Biking: 87, 162; do-it-yourself tour, 175; Haarlem, 136; parking garage, 15; rentals, 162; tours, 175
Blauwbrug: 127
Bloemenmarkt: 31
Boat tours: 164, 173–174
Bookstores: 160, 170
Boom Chicago: 172
Bulldog Café and Coffeeshop: 33–34, 75, 173
Burgomaster of Delft and His Daughter (Steen): 44–45
Buses: 163–164; to/from airport, 158
Business hours: 160

C

Cabs: 164; to/from airport, 158
Cafés: about, 144–146; listings, 149–151
Café 't Mandje: 81
Canal bikes: 174
Canal boats: 164, 173–174
Canal House (Het Grachtenhuis): 127
Canal Mansion, Herengracht: 9, 126
Canals of Amsterdam: 6–7, 10, 15, 18, 20; maps, 4–5, 16–17, 88–89. *See also specific canals*
Cannabis College: 83
Car travel: 164–165
Cell (mobile) phones: 166
Centraal Train Station: 14–15, 158–159; shopping, 169
Central Amsterdam: 7, 10; eating, 149–150; maps, 16–17, 117; sights, 116–120; sleeping, 137, 141; walking tour, 13–34. *See also* Red Light District

Central Library: 9, 133, 161
Cheese: 90, 136, 147
Churches and cathedrals: De Papegaai Hidden Church, 25; English Reformed Church, 27–28; Grote Kerk (Haarlem), 134; New Church, 23–25, 116; Old Church, 74; St. Nicholas Church, 15; Westerkerk, 94–95, 121
Civic Guard Gallery: 26–27
Climate: 156
Concertgebouw: 123, 171
Condomerie: 71
Consulates: 165
Corrie ten Boom House (Harlem): 136
Coster Diamonds: 123–124
Credit cards: 157
Cuisine: 147–148; ethnic, 148; traditional Dutch, 147–148. *See also* Eating
Currency and exchange: 157
Customs regulations: 170–171

D

Damrak: 15, 18–19
Damrak Sex Museum: 18, 120
Dam Square: 19, 22–25, 86
Day trips: 134–136
De Bijenkorf: 22, 160
Debit cards: 157
De Hortus Botanical Garden: 130
Delft: 136
Delft Blue Shop: 33
Delftware: 33, 52, 170
De Negen Straatjes: 25, 169
De Papegaai Hidden Church: 25
Department stores: 169
De Wallen: *See* Red Light District
Diamonds: 9, 123–124, 129
Dining: *See* Eating
Discounts: 167
Dollebegijnensteeg: 75–76
Dutch East India Company: 20–21, 79, 134
Dutch Golden Age: *See* Golden Age
Dutch phrases: 177
Dutch Resistance Museum: 8, 132
Dutch Theater: 9, 131–132

E

Eating: 143–153; Anne Frank House, 102; listings, 149–151; map, 152–153; price code, 144; Rijksmuseum, 37; tipping, 161; Van Gogh Museum, 54
Edam: 136
Eerste Leliedwarsstraat: 96–97
Egelantiersgracht: 97
Electricity: 160
Electric Ladyland: 98
Elements of Nature: 71
Embassies: 165
Emergencies: 165, 168
English Reformed Church: 27–28
Enkhuizen: 136
Erotic Museum: 82, 120
Euro currency: 157
Excursion areas: 134–136
EYE Film Institute Netherlands: 9, 134

F

Feast of St. Nicholas, The (Steen): 42–45
Flea Market, Waterlooplein: 127, 170
Flower Market: 31
Frank, Anne: 101–112; statue of, 93. *See also* Anne Frank House
Frans Hals Museum (Haarlem): 135

G

Gables: about, 91
Garden of Saint Paul's Hospital (Van Gogh): 66
Gassan Diamonds: 129
Gauguin's Chair (Van Gogh): 64
Golden Age: 20–21, 39; Rijksmuseum, 37–52; ruffs, 43

"Golden Curve": 32
Great Synagogue: 130
Grey Area Coffeeshop: 90, 92, 173
Grote Kerk (Haarlem): 134
Guided tours: *See* Tours

H

Haarlem: 135–136
Hague, The: 136
Hals, Frans: 38–40; Museum (Haarlem), 135
Hash, Marijuana, and Hemp Museum: 9, 84
Heineken Experience: 124
Helpful hints: 160–161
Hemp Gallery: 84
Herengracht: 32, 92
Herengracht Canal Mansion: 9, 126
Hermitage Amsterdam: 8, 129–130
Herring stands: 31–32, 93, 149
Historic Triangle: 136
History of Amsterdam: 20–21
Hollandsche Schouwburg: 9, 131
Homomonument: 93
Hotels: *See* Sleeping
Houseboat Museum: 9, 120–121
House of Bols: Cocktail & Genever Experience: 124

I

Irish pubs: 71
Isaac and Rebecca (Rembrandt): 46
Itineraries: 10, 12

J

Jazz music: 172
Jenever: 146, 170
Jeremiah Lamenting the Destruction of Jerusalem (Rembrandt): 51
Jewish Bride, The (Rembrandt): 46
Jewish Historical Museum: 9, 130–131
Jewish Quarter: 127–128
Joods Historisch Museum: 9, 130–131
Jordaan: 85–100; eating, 150–151; map, 88–89; shopping, 169; walking tour, 86–100. *See also* Anne Frank House

K

Kalverstraat: 25, 26, 29; eating, 149; shopping, 169
Kalvertoren: 29
Keizersgracht: 93
Keizersgracht Bridge: 93
Keukenhof: 136
Koningsplein: 31–32
Koninklijk Huis: *See* Royal Palace
Korte Stormsteeg: 81

L

Language: 160; Dutch phrases, 177
Laundry: 161
Leiden: 136
Leidseplein: 9, 33–34, 125; eating, 151; nightlife, 171, 172; sleeping, 141
Leidsestraat: 32–33
Leliegracht: 92–93
Little Street, The (Vermeer): 42
"Little Venice": 79
Love Letter, The (Vermeer): 41–42
Luggage lockers: 159

M

Magere Brug: 128
Magna Plaza Shopping Center: 86, 169
Maps: Amsterdam, 4–5; Amsterdam city walk, 16–17; Amsterdam's neighborhoods, 7; Amsterdam's sights, 114–115; to buy, 160; Central Amsterdam, 117; eating, 152–153; Jordaan, 88–89; Red Light District, 72–73; Rijksmuseum, 36; Southeast Amsterdam, 128; Southwest Amsterdam, 122

Maria Trip (Rembrandt): 50
Marijuana: 83–84, 173; Bulldog Café and Coffeeshop, 33–34, 75, 173; Grey Area Coffeeshop, 90, 92, 173; Hash, Marijuana, and Hemp Museum, 9, 84; Paradox Coffeeshop, 98, 173. *See also* Smartshops
Maritime Museum: 8, 133–134
Markets: 170; Flower Market, 31; Haarlem, 135; Waterlooplein, 127, 170
Medical help: 165, 168
Melkweg: 33, 172
Merry Drinker, The (Hals): 38
Merry Family, The (Steen): 44
Metric system: 161
Metro: 163–164
Militiaman Holding a Berkemeyer (Hals): 38
Milkmaid, The (Vermeer): 40–41
Mint Tower: 29
Mobile phones: 166
Molsteeg: 86–87
Money: 157
Money belts: 157
Moses and Aaron Church: 127
Movie theaters: 172–173
Multatuli (a.k.a. Eduard Douwes Dekker): 89
Munttoren: 29
Museum Het Rembrandthuis: 9, 128–129
Museum of Bags and Purses: 126
Museumplein: 8, 123–124; eating, 151; map, 122; shopping, 169–170; sleeping, 142
Museums: daily reminder, 11; Amstelkring Museum, 8, 77–78, 118–119; Amsterdam Museum, 8, 25–27, 118; Canal House, 127; Damrak Sex Museum, 18, 120; Dutch Resistance Museum, 8, 132; Erotic Museum, 82, 120; general tips, 12, 167–168; Hash, Marijuana, and Hemp Museum, 9, 84; Herengracht Canal Mansion, 9, 126; Hermitage Amsterdam, 8, 129–130; Houseboat Museum, 9, 120–121; Jewish Historical Museum, 130–131; Museum Het Rembrandthuis, 9, 128–129; NEMO (National Center for Science and Technology), 133; Netherlands Maritime Museum, 8, 133–134; Pipe Museum, 126–127; Stedelijk Museum, 8, 123; Tropical Museum, 9, 132. *See also* Anne Frank House; Rijksmuseum; Van Gogh Museum
Music: 171–172

N

National Center for Science and Technology (NEMO): 133
National Holocaust Memorial: 131–132
National Monument: 24–25
Nederlands Scheepvaartmuseum: 8, 133–134
Neighborhoods: 6–7, 10; map, 7. *See also specific neighborhoods*
NEMO (National Center for Science and Technology): 133, 161
Netherlands: overview, 125
Netherlands Maritime Museum: 8, 133–134
New Church: 23–25, 116; concerts, 171
New Synagogue: 131
Nieuwe Kerk: 23–25, 116; concerts, 171
Nieuwe Leliestraat: 96
Nightlife: 171–173
Night Watch, The (Rembrandt): 47–48
Nine Little Streets: 25, 169
Northeast Amsterdam: 10; sights, 133–134

O
Old Church: 74, 161; concerts, 171–172
Old Church Tower at Nuenen, The (Van Gogh): 58
Old wooden house: 79
Openbare Bibliotheek Amsterdam: 9, 133
Oude Kerk: 74, 161; concerts, 171–172
Oude Leliestraat: 90, 92
Oudezijds Achterburgwal: 81–83
Oudezijds Voorburgwal: 77–78
Our Lord in the Attic/Museum: 8, 77–78, 118–119

P
Paddleboats: 174
Paradiso: 172
Paradox Coffeeshop: 98, 173
Passenger Terminal Amsterdam (PTA): 159
Passports: 156
P.C. Hooftstraat: 170
Pedestrian safety: 161
Petrus en Paulus Kerk: 25
Phone numbers, useful: 165
Phones: 165–166
Pickpockets: 70, 76, 168
Picnicking: 146–147
Pietà (after Delacroix) (Van Gogh): 67
Pill Bridge: 77
Pipe Museum: 126–127
Planning tips: 10, 12, 156
Police: 165
Portrait of a Couple (Hals): 38–40
Portuguese Synagogue: 9, 131
Potato Eaters, The (Van Gogh): 57
Princess Juliana Daycare: 77
Prinsengracht: 94–96
Prostitution: 78–79; Red Light Secrets Museum of Prostitution, 120
Prostitution Information Center: 76

R
Raven, Mark: 86
Reader feedback: 176
Red Cabbages and Onions (Van Gogh): 59
Red Light District (Amsterdam): 8, 69–84, 119; map, 72–73; nightlife, 171–172; orientation, 8, 70; walking tour, 70–84
Red Light District (Haarlem): 136
Red Light Secrets Museum of Prostitution: 120
Rembrandtplein: 125–126; nightlife, 171
Rembrandt van Rijn: biographical sketch, 45–46; burial site, 94–95, 121; House, 9, 128–129; at Rijksmuseum, 45–51
Rental properties: 139
"Restaurant Row": 33, 151
Restaurants: about, 144; cuisine, 147–148; listings, 149–151; map, 152–153
Reypenaer cheese shop: 90
Ricksteves.com: 176
Rijksmuseum: 35–52, 121; map, 36; orientation, 8, 36–37; self-guided tour, 37–52
Rijsttafel: 18, 148, 149
Rock music: 172
Rotterdam: 136
Royal Palace: 9, 23, 116
Ruffs: about, 43

S
St. Andrew's Courtyard: 98, 100
St. Nicholas Church: 15
Schiphol Airport: 158
Schokland: 136
Schuttersgalerij: 26–27
Seasons: 156
Self-Portrait (Rembrandt): 49–50
Self-Portrait as an Painter (Van Gogh): 59
Self-Portrait as the Apostle Paul (Rembrandt): 49

Self-Portrait with Gray Felt Hat (Van Gogh): 60
Self-Portrait with Straw Hat (Van Gogh): 59
Sensi Seed Bank Store: 84
Sex museums: 120; Damrak Sex Museum, 18, 120; Erotic Museum, 82, 120
Sex shops: 71, 74
Sheaf-Binder, The, after Millet (Van Gogh): 66
Shopping: 169–171; hours, 160, 169; VAT refunds, 170
Sights (sightseeing): 13–136; at a glance, 8–9; advance tickets, 167–168; daily reminder, 11; general tips, 12, 167–168; itineraries, 10, 12; passes, 12, 167–168. *See also* Walking tours; *and specific sights*
Singel Canal: 20, 87–90
Sint-Andrieshof: 98, 100
Sleeping: 137–142; budget tips, 139; listings, 140–142; price code, 139; reservations, 12, 138; typical hotel room, 138
Smartphones: 166
Smartshops: 33, 71
Smoking: tobacco, 146. *See also* Marijuana
Southeast Amsterdam: 10; map, 128; sights, 127–132
Southern Canal Belt: 10; sights, 125–127; sleeping, 137, 142
Southwest Amsterdam: 10; eating, 151; map, 122; shopping, 169–170; sights, 121–125; sleeping, 137, 142. *See also* Rijksmuseum; Van Gogh Museum
Souvenirs, shopping for: 170
Sower, The (Van Gogh): 62, 64
Spiegelkwartier: 169–170
Spui: nightlife, 171
Spui Square: 29; eating, 149
Stadsschouwburg Theater: 33
Stedelijk Museum: 8, 123; late-night hours, 173
Steen, Jan: 42–45
Still Life with Bible (Van Gogh): 57–58
Stock Exchange: 19
"Stopera": 127
Sunflowers (Van Gogh): 62
Syndics, The (Rembrandt): 46–47

T

Tarantino, Quentin: 71
Tassenmuseum Hendrikje: 126
Taxes: VAT refunds, 170
Taxis: 164; to/from airport, 158
Telephone numbers, useful: 165
Telephones: 165–166
Teylers Museum (Haarlem): 135–136
Theater: 172
Theatre Casa Rosso: 82
Theft alert: 70, 76, 168
Time zone: 160
Tipping: 161
Torensluis Bridge: 87–90
Tour guides: 174
Tourist information: 156, 160
Tours: 174–175; by bike, 175; by boat, 164, 173–174
Train station: *See* Centraal Train Station
Train travel: 156; to/from airport, 158
Trams: 159, 163–164
Transportation: 161–165; to Amsterdam, 158–159
Tropical Museum: 9, 132
"Tulip mania": 31, 44
Tuschinski Theater: 126, 173
Tweede Egelantiers: 97

U

Uitkrant: 171
Utrecht: 136

V

Van Gogh, Vincent: biographical sketch, 55–56; at Rijksmuseum, 52. *See also* Van Gogh Museum
Van Gogh Museum: 53–68, 123, 170; late-night hours, 173; orientation, 8, 54; self-guided tour, 55–68
VAT refunds: 170
Vermeer, Johannes: 40–42
Verzetsmuseum: 8, 132
View of Houses in Delft (Vermeer): 42
Vijzelstraat: 29
Vondelpark: 8, 124–125

W

Walking tours: central city, 13–34; guided, 174; Jordaan, 85–100; Red Light District, 69–84
Wardens of the Amsterdam Drapers Guild (Rembrandt): 46–47
Warmoesstraat: 70–71, 74
Waterlooplein Flea Market: 127, 170
Weather: 156
Websites, helpful: 156
West Amsterdam: 10; eating, 150–151; shopping, 169; sights, 120–121; sleeping, 137, 140–141. *See also* Anne Frank House; Jordaan
Westerkerk: 94–95, 121, 161; concerts, 171
Westermarkt Square: 93
Wheatfield with a Reaper (Van Gogh): 66–67
Wheatfield with Crows (Van Gogh): 68
Wi-Fi: 166
Wijde Kerksteeg: 71, 74
Willet-Holthuysen Museum: 9, 126
Winston Hotel: 71
Woman Reading a Letter (Vermeer): 41
Woonbootmuseum (Houseboat Museum): 9, 120–121World War II: 21, 127, 131, 136; Dutch Resistance Museum, 8, 132; National Holocaust Memorial, 131–132; National Monument, 24–25. *See also* Anne Frank House

Y

Yellow Bike Guided Tours: 176
Yellow House, The (Van Gogh): 60–61
Young Woman in Fantasy Costume (Rembrandt): 50

Z

Zaanse Schans: 136
Zeedijk: 78–81
Zuiderzee: 15, 20

PHOTO CREDITS

Cover
© Vitalyedush | Dreamstime.com

Table of Contents
p. 2, right The Yorck Project*, commons.wikimedia.org

Rijksmuseum Tour
All photos courtesy of the Rijksmuseum, except p. 37, left & right © 123rf.com; p. 39, PD-US/PD-Art, commons.wikimedia.org; p. 43, Rick Steves.
Additional Rijksmuseum image information:
p. 35 Frans Hals, A Militiaman Holding a Berkemeyer, Known as the 'Merry Drinker', c. 1628 - c. 1630. Rijksmuseum, Amsterdam; p. 40, left Johannes Vermeer, The milkmaid, c. 1660. Purchased with the support of the Vereniging Rembrandt; p 40, right Johannes Vermeer, Woman Reading a Letter, c. 1663. On loan from the City of Amsterdam (A. van der Hoop Bequest); p. 42, left Johannes Vermeer, The Love Letter, c. 1669 - c. 1670. Rijksmuseum, Amsterdam, Purchased with the support of the Vereniging Rembrandt; p. 42, right Johannes Vermeer, View of Houses in Delft, Known as The Little Street, c. 1658. Gift of H.W.A. Deterding, London; p. 44, left Jan Havicksz. Steen, Adolf and Catharina Croeser, Known as 'The Burgomaster of Delft and his Daughter', 1655. Purchased with the support of the Nationaal Aankoopfonds of the Ministerie van OCenW, the BankGiro Loterij, the Stichting Nationaal Fonds Kunstbezit, the Mondriaan Stichting, the VSBfonds, the Vereniging Rembrandt, with additional funding from the Prins Bernhard Cultuurfonds and the Rijksmuseum Fonds; p. 44, right Jan Havicksz. Steen, The Feast of St Nicholas, 1665 – 1668. Rijksmuseum, Amsterdam; p. 45 Jan Havicksz. Steen, The Merry Family, 1668. On loan from the City of Amsterdam (A. van der Hoop Bequest); p. 47, left Rembrandt Harmensz. van Rijn, Portrait of a Couple as Isaac and Rebecca, known as 'The Jewish Bride', c. 1665 - c. 1669. On loan from the City of Amsterdam (A. van der Hoop Bequest); p. 47, right Rembrandt Harmensz. van Rijn, Militia Company of District II under the Command of Captain Frans Banninck Cocq, Known as the 'Night Watch', 1642. On loan from the City of Amsterdam; p. 49, left Rembrandt Harmensz. van Rijn, Self-portrait, c. 1628. Purchased with the support of the Vereniging Rembrandt, the Stichting tot Bevordering van de Belangen van het Rijksmuseum and the ministerie van CRM; p. 49, right Rembrandt Harmensz. van Rijn, Jeremiah Lamenting the Destruction of Jerusalem, 1630. Purchased with the support of private collectors, the Vereniging Rembrandt and the Stichting tot Bevordering van de Belangen van het Rijksmuseum; p. 50, left Rembrandt Harmensz. van Rijn, Portrait of a Woman, Possibly Maria Trip, 1639. Rijksmuseum, Amsterdam, On loan from the Familie Van Weede Stichting; p. 50, right Rembrandt Harmensz. van Rijn, Self Portrait as the Apostle Paul, 1661. De Bruijn-van der Leeuw Bequest, Muri, Switzerland; p. 51 Bartholomeus van der Helst, Banquet at the Crossbowmen's Guild in Celebration

of the Treaty of Münster, 1648. On loan from the City of Amsterdam; p. 52, left Pieter Claesz., Still Life with a Turkey Pie, 1627. Rijksmuseum, Amsterdam, Purchased with the support of the Vereniging Rembrandt and the Stichting tot Bevordering van de Belangen van het Rijksmuseump.

Van Gogh Museum Tour
All photos from Google Art Project, commons.wikimedia.org, except p. 54 & p. 64, Rick Steves; p. 55 & p. 59, right, © Peter Horree / Alamy; p. 60, left, The Yorck Project*, commons.wikimedia.org

Anne Frank House Tour
p. 104, left, © Everett Collection Inc / Alamy, right, © Daily Mail/Rex / Alamy;p. 105, © BRIAN HARRIS / Alamy; p. 107 © Pictorial Press Ltd / Alamy; p. 111 © epa european pressphoto agency b.v. / Alamy

Additional images by Dominic Arizona Bonuccelli, Rich Earl, Tom Griffin, Jennifer Hauseman, Gene Openshaw, Rick Steves, Gretchen Strauch, and Laura VanDeventer

Photos are used by permission and are the property of the original copyright owners.

* Additional Yorck Project information: The work of art depicted in this image and the reproduction thereof are in the public domain worldwide. The reproduction is part of a collection of reproductions compiled by The Yorck Project. The compilation copyright is held by Zenodot Verlagsgesellschaft mbH and licensed under the GNU Free Documentation License. The Yorck Project: 10.000 Meisterwerke der Malerei. DVD-ROM, 2002. ISBN 3936122202. Distributed by DIRECTMEDIA Publishing GmbH.

Unless otherwise noted, copyrights apply to photographs of artwork.

Start your trip at

Our website enhances this book and turns

Explore Europe

At ricksteves.com you can browse through thousands of articles, videos, photos and radio interviews, plus find a wealth of money-saving travel tips for planning your dream trip. And with our mobile-friendly website, you can easily access all this great travel information anywhere you go.

TV Shows

Preview the places you'll visit by watching entire half-hour episodes of Rick Steves' Europe (choose from all 100 shows) on-demand, for free.

ricksteves.com

your travel dreams into affordable reality

Radio Interviews

Enjoy ready access to Rick's vast library of radio interviews covering travel tips and cultural insights that relate specifically to your Europe travel plans.

Travel Forums

Learn, ask, share! Our online community of savvy travelers is a great resource for first-time travelers to Europe, as well as seasoned pros. You'll find forums on each country, plus travel tips and restaurant/hotel reviews. You can even ask one of our well-traveled staff to chime in with an opinion.

Travel News

Subscribe to our free Travel News e-newsletter, and get monthly updates from Rick on what's happening in Europe.

Audio Europe™

Rick's Free Travel App

Get your FREE Rick Steves Audio Europe™ app to enjoy…

- Dozens of self-guided tours of Europe's top museums, sights and historic walks
- Hundreds of tracks filled with cultural insights and sightseeing tips from Rick's radio interviews
- All organized into handy geographic playlists
- For Apple and Android

With Rick whispering in your ear, Europe gets even better.

Find out more at ricksteves.com

Pack Light and Right

Gear up for your next adventure at ricksteves.com

Light Luggage

Pack light and right with Rick Steves' affordable, custom-designed rolling carry-on bags, backpacks, day packs and shoulder bags.

Accessories

From packing cubes to moneybelts and beyond, Rick has personally selected the travel goodies that will help your trip go smoother.

Shop at ricksteves.com

Rick Steves has

Experience maximum Europe

Save time and energy

This guidebook is your independent-travel toolkit. But for all it delivers, it's still up to you to devote the time and energy it takes to manage the preparation and logistics that are essential for a happy trip. If that's a hassle, there's a solution.

Rick Steves Tours

A Rick Steves tour takes you to Europe's most interesting places with great guides and small groups

great tours, too!

with minimum stress

of 28 or less. We follow Rick's favorite itineraries, ride in comfy buses, stay in family-run hotels, and bring you intimately close to the Europe you've traveled so far to see. Most importantly, we take away the logistical headaches so you can focus on the fun.

Join the fun

This year we'll take thousands of free-spirited travelers—nearly half

of them repeat customers—along with us on four dozen different itineraries, from Ireland to Italy to Athens. Is a Rick Steves tour the right fit for your travel dreams? Find out at ricksteves.com, where you can also request Rick's latest tour catalog.

Europe is best experienced with happy travel partners. We hope you can join us.

See our itineraries at ricksteves.com

A Guide for Every Trip

BEST OF GUIDES

Full color easy-to-scan format, focusing on Europe's most popular destinations and sights.

Best of France
Best of Germany
Best of England
Best of Europe
Best of Ireland
Best of Italy
Best of Spain

COMPREHENSIVE GUIDES

City, country, and regional guides with detailed coverage for a multi-week trip exploring iconic sights and more.

Amsterdam & the Netherlands
Barcelona
Belgium: Bruges, Brussels, Antwerp & Ghent
Berlin
Budapest
Croatia & Slovenia
Eastern Europe
England
Florence & Tuscany
France
Germany
Great Britain
Greece: Athens & the Peloponnese
Iceland
Ireland
Istanbul
Italy
London
Paris
Portugal
Prague & the Czech Republic
Provence & the French Riviera
Rome
Scandinavia
Scotland
Spain
Switzerland
Venice
Vienna, Salzburg & Tirol

Rick Steves guidebooks are published by Avalon Travel, an imprint of Perseus Books, a Hachette Book Group company.

POCKET GUIDES

Amsterdam
Athens
Barcelona
Florence
Italy's Cinque Terre
London
Munich & Salzburg
Paris
Prague
Rome
Venice
Vienna

SNAPSHOT GUIDES

Focused single-destination coverage.

Basque Country: Spain & France
Copenhagen & the Best of Denmark
Dublin
Dubrovnik
Edinburgh
Hill Towns of Central Italy
Krakow, Warsaw & Gdansk
Lisbon
Loire Valley
Madrid & Toledo
Milan & the Italian Lakes District
Naples & the Amalfi Coast
Northern Ireland
Normandy
Norway
Reykjavik
Sevilla, Granada & Southern Spain
St. Petersburg, Helsinki & Tallinn
Stockholm

CRUISE PORTS GUIDES

Reference for cruise ports of call.

Mediterranean Cruise Ports
Northern European Cruise Ports

TRAVEL SKILLS & CULTURE

Europe 101
European Christmas
European Easter
European Festivals
Europe Through the Back Door
Postcards from Europe
Travel as a Political Act

PHRASE BOOKS & DICTIONARIES

French
French, Italian & German
German
Italian
Portuguese
Spanish

PLANNING MAPS

Britain, Ireland & London
Europe
France & Paris
Germany, Austria & Switzerland
Ireland
Italy
Spain & Portugal

Rick Steves books are available from your favorite bookseller.
Many guides are available as ebooks.

Avalon Travel
An imprint of Perseus Books
A Hachette Book Group company

1700 Fourth Street
Berkeley, CA 94710

Text © 2017 by Rick Steves' Europe, Inc. All rights reserved.
Maps © 2017 by Rick Steves' Europe, Inc. All rights reserved.

Printed in China by RR Donnelley
Second edition
First printing September 2017

ISBN 978-1-63121-627-5

For the latest on Rick's lectures, guidebooks, tours, public radio show, and public television series, contact Rick Steves' Europe, 130 Fourth Avenue North, Edmonds, WA 98020, tel. 425/771-8303, fax 425/771-0833, ricksteves.com, or rick@ricksteves.com.

Rick Steves' Europe
Managing Editor: Jennifer Madison Davis
Special Publications Manager: Risa Laib
Editors: Glenn Eriksen, Tom Griffin, Katherine Gustafson, Mary E. Keils, Suzanne Kotz, Cathy Lu, Carrie Shepherd
Editorial & Production Assistant: Jessica Shaw
Editorial Intern: Meesha Sundarum
Researchers: Tom Griffin, Sandra Hundacker
Graphic Content Director: Sandra Hundacker
Maps & Graphics: David C. Hoerlein, Lauren Mills, Mary Rostad

Avalon Travel
Senior Editor and Series Manager: Madhu Prasher
Editor: Jamie Andrade
Associate Editor: Sierra Machado
Copy Editor: Maggie Ryan
Proofreader: Janet Walden
Indexer: Stephen Callahan
Production & Typesetting: Christine DeLorenzo
Cover Design: Kimberly Glyder Design
Interior Design: Darren Alessi
Maps & Graphics: Kat Bennett, Lohnes + Wright

Although the author and publisher have made every effort to provide accurate, up-to-date information, they accept no responsibility for loss, injury, bad herring, or inconvenience sustained by any person using this book.

ABOUT THE AUTHORS

Rick Steves

Since 1973, Rick has spent about four months a year exploring Europe. His mission: to empower Americans to have European trips that are fun, affordable, and culturally broadening. Rick produces a best-selling guidebook series, a public television series, and a public radio show, and organizes small-group tours that take over 20,000 travelers to Europe annually. He does all of this with the help of a hardworking, well-traveled staff of 100 at Rick Steves' Europe in Edmonds, Washington, near Seattle. When not on the road, Rick is active in his church and with advocacy groups focused on economic justice, drug policy reform, and ending hunger. To recharge, Rick plays piano, relaxes at his family cabin in the Cascade Mountains, and spends time with his partner Trish, son Andy, and daughter Jackie. Find out more about Rick at www.ricksteves.com and on Facebook.

Gene Openshaw

Gene has co-authored a dozen *Rick Steves* books, specializing in writing walks and tours of Europe's cities, museums, and cultural sights. He also contributes to Rick's public television series, produces tours for Rick Steves Audio Europe, and is a regular guest on Rick's public radio show. Outside of the travel world, Gene has co-authored *The Seattle Joke Book.* As a composer, Gene has written a full-length opera called *Matter* (soundtrack available on Amazon), a violin sonata, and dozens of songs. He lives near Seattle with his daughter, enjoys giving presentations on art and history, and roots for the Mariners in good times and bad.

FOLDOUT COLOR MAP

The foldout map on the opposite page includes:

- **A map of Amsterdam on one side**
- **Maps of Amsterdam and the Netherlands on the other side**